ONE
BOLD
MOVE
A DAY

ONE BOLD MOVE A DAY

MEANINGFUL ACTIONS WOMEN CAN
TAKE TO FULFILL THEIR LEADERSHIP
AND CAREER POTENTIAL

SHANNA A. HOCKING

Founder, One Bold Move a Day

Mc
Graw
Hill

NEW YORK   CHICAGO   SAN FRANCISCO   ATHENS   LONDON
MADRID   MEXICO CITY   MILAN   NEW DELHI
SINGAPORE   SYDNEY   TORONTO

1 2 3 4 5 6 7 8 9   LCR   27 26 25 24 23 22

ISBN   978-1-264-27807-7
MHID   1-264-27807-1

e-ISBN   978-1-264-27808-4
e-MHID   1-264-27808-X

Library of Congress Cataloging-in-Publication Data

Names: Hocking, Shanna A., author.
Title: One bold move a day : meaningful actions women can take to fulfill
   their leadership and career potential / Shanna A. Hocking.
Description: 1 Edition. | New York : McGraw Hill, [2023] | Includes
   bibliographical references and index.
Identifiers: LCCN 2022030511 (print) | LCCN 2022030512 (ebook) |
   ISBN 9781264278077 (hardback) | ISBN 9781264278084 (ebook)
Subjects: LCSH: Leadership in women. | Career development. | Self-confidence. |
   Self-actualization (Psychology)
Classification: LCC HD6054.3 .H63 2023 (print) | LCC HD6054.3 (ebook) |
   DDC 658.4/092—dc23/eng/20220908
LC record available at https://lccn.loc.gov/2022030511
LC ebook record available at https://lccn.loc.gov/2022030512

McGraw Hill books are available at special quantity discounts to use as premiums and sales promotions or for use in corporate training programs. To contact a representative, please visit the Contact Us pages at www.mhprofessional.com.

McGraw Hill is committed to making our products accessible to all learners. To learn more about the available support and accommodations we offer, please contact us at accessibility@mheducation.com. We also participate in the Access Text Network (www.accesstext.org), and ATN members may submit requests through ATN.

For my mom,

Thank you for all the times growing up

when you sat next to me

while I was stuck in my writing.

You always believed in me.

This is for you.

Contents

CONTENTS

Introduction

Who do *you* want to become?

That's a pretty big question, but the good news is you don't have to know the answer to that just yet. After all, this question is likely why you're here.

Looking back to where I started, I was desperate for someone to show me how to advance in my career, develop as a leader, and grow as a person, so I listened to anyone willing to share advice and read every business and personal development book I could get my hands on.

I pursued my dream career and life, learned from many mistakes, and celebrated many successes. Along the way, I also ended up with a strong network and large bookshelf. But something was still missing. I kept searching for a roadmap that showed me it was okay to be ambitious, that being grateful *and* wanting more wasn't a paradox, and that I wasn't alone.

That's where my idea to start taking one Bold Move a day began. I decided it was time to achieve what I had never thought was possible for myself—and did that with a challenge and a reminder that I needed to put myself out there and follow through, though I will admit that this wasn't concrete or conscious at first.

Over time, that changed. I realized that the more intentional I was with this commitment to myself to make one Bold Move a day, even if it was the smallest step in the direction I wanted to go, the stronger, more confident, more compassionate, and more successful I was—and it inspired others. And the easier it became to truly celebrate my progress, too.

Today, as a leadership consultant and philanthropic advisor who spent 20 years raising hundreds of millions of dollars and leading large teams in multibillion-dollar nonprofit organizations, I want to share everything I've learned up to this point (often the hard way) with you.

One Bold Move a Day is the book I had been looking for all this time—and I hope it can be your missing link to create the success you and I both know is possible for you.

WHAT DOES IT MEAN TO MAKE ONE BOLD MOVE A DAY?

When you think about Bold Moves, you might be thinking BOLD MOVES.

Yes, a Bold Move can be something you do that merits an all-caps text to a friend. But the reality is a Bold Move isn't always going to be something as significant as moving to a new city or taking a new job. Your one Bold Move might be asking for the server to bring the mustard you wanted instead of quietly wishing they had. Or maybe it's saying hello to a person you pass on the street. It might be speaking up in a meeting, disagreeing with someone more senior than you, or negotiating your salary to get paid what you're worth.

A Bold Move is one that *challenges you to grow*. Sometimes it's about capitalizing on an opportunity, and sometimes it's about creating that opportunity for yourself. A Bold Move might look like a radical shift in your life, or it might be barely noticeable to others. Bold Moves can happen at work or at home, in friendships, relationships, and even in loving yourself.

Thinking about your Bold Move may make your heart beat a little quicker—and there's likely a voice in your head that tells you not to do it, and that's okay. Making a Bold Move requires intentionality, courage, and follow-through.

A Bold Move for you might not be the same as someone else's. No one gets to judge your Bold Move and whether it's good enough. Including you. You have to face the fear you're feeling and learn to do things while you're afraid.

With each Bold Move, you'll grow stronger, more confident, and more compassionate. And you'll inspire others, sometimes in ways you'll never know and other times in ways you'll be grateful to discover. No matter the case, you deserve to achieve your goals. You deserve to advance your career. You deserve great things. And you have the power to do all of this for yourself.

With one Bold Move a day.

It wasn't always like this for me, though.

Early in my career, I walked into the office wearing a suit, a smile, and ready to share all of my ideas. And share I did. I'd speak up in meetings, comment on colleagues' strategies, and raise my hand for new projects. Though what I did well helped me get promoted, it also became a magnet for other people's opinions. I heard the whispers behind my back, and there were plenty of comments to my face. They were along the lines of, "Who does she think she is?" "She shouldn't be so out there." "She needs to take it down a bit."

I internalized the commentary. It showed up in second-guessing myself or holding back an opinion. Over time, I minimized my own strengths in order to make others more comfortable. I didn't even realize I was doing this. For years. But with help from an executive coach and loved ones, I slowly regained the power of being the best version of myself. I learned how to work through fears and rise anyway. I later realized other people's reactions often had nothing to do with me.

This is where *One Bold Move a Day* comes from. I wanted other women to proudly share their best selves as they worked to achieve their goals. You can lead yourself and others with joy through intentionally making Bold Moves.

ABOUT THIS BOOK

When I wrote this book for you, I wanted to support you in fulfilling your potential both personally and professionally. Each chapter focuses on a different priority area to help you advance your career, grow as a person, and develop as a leader.

At the end of each chapter, you will find three Bold Moves for you to make now, so you can apply what you've learned and begin to take meaningful actions to fulfill your potential.

WHAT *ONE BOLD MOVE A DAY* WILL TEACH YOU

Through this book, you will learn what is possible for yourself. You'll be reminded of your existing strengths and cultivate new ones. You'll understand that even the smallest step in the direction you want to go will get you closer to your goals and give you courage and energy to put yourself out there to try something new.

The reality is that sometimes the small things you do each day will end up leading to very big things. That's how movements get started. You might start the first step in a project you've been thinking about for years. You might make one new connection at an event. You might support one person's goals or get a new job. Whatever it is, one single Bold Move can change the trajectory of your career and your success, as long as you get started.

As for the right time? Well, there will never really be a perfect moment. You just have to start somewhere, so why not start right here and right now?

Bold Mindset Shifts

To prepare yourself to make one Bold Move a day, it helps to get into the right mindset—the right *four* mindsets, actually! The four bold mindset shifts include:

1. Gratitude Mindset
2. *And* Mindset
3. Happiness Mindset
4. Progress Mindset

Each of these four mindsets individually plays a special role in the process of continuously showing up for yourself and others. They also represent a significant shift in how I approached my work and life, and they will provide you with the context and encouragement to successfully put yourself out there and follow through.

Each mindset contributes in a different way to your success, but they all complement each other and together they will become the foundation to your Bold Move Mindset. Because even when your Bold Moves create your path, things may not always turn out as you've planned. There will be days when it may not even feel like you're moving forward, and in that case, you need to consider your growth with the appropriate mindset. Let's dive deeper into each of these mindsets to know when and how each can be used.

GRATITUDE MINDSET

I can still remember the day I walked into work and learned I was being reorged. My job responsibilities shifted, and part of my team was moved to another reporting line. Though, looking back now, I see there had been a few warning signs, in the moment I felt completely caught off guard. Our team had excelled, and I had been recognized for my leadership—but I had forgotten the importance of proactively talking about these accomplishments and took for granted that others were aware of what we had been doing. My first mistake was assuming that I would be noticed if I worked hard, and my second mistake was starting to withdraw at work, and worse, chatting behind closed doors.

I know this was not ideal. As the leader of a team, I had even more responsibility to help my staff members navigate this transition, especially those who also had their jobs changed unexpectedly. I felt like a failure for not protecting them and for not protecting myself.

I realized I needed to do something to help regain my sense of control of the situation.

In reading articles and books on facing change at work, I came across many suggestions and concepts to try. One that I kept seeing was a "gratitude list," which I will fully admit I scoffed a bit about at first. I didn't think that something so simple could really help change my life. I wasn't one of those woo-woo people, and I was far too realistic to see only the positive. Plus, when my work life turned upside down, the last thing I felt was *grateful*. Of course, I was grateful for my health and my family, but those things felt too substantial for this exercise and didn't address the problems I was facing at work.

Despite my initial pushback, I decided to focus on being grateful for the good things that happened each day to keep me grounded in the moment I was in. It took me a while to get started. I had trouble noticing the good things. One of my earliest notes included appreciation for rain boots. Another day I was grateful for the conversation at family dinner. As I practiced gratitude with more intention, my notes changed to the beauty of individual moments spent with family and friends, sharing ideas in meetings, working on new projects, and more.

When I sat down to review my gratitude journal to write this chapter, my tears filled my eyes when I read one entry: "I can feel gratitude changing me." It made me realize that it can be tough for negative emotions to flourish when you're consciously keeping track of things that bring you joy.

Gratitude comes in all forms and sizes. There is no judgment if your list includes the latte from your favorite coffee shop or an extra delicious piece of cake. Like any Bold Move, it's about recognizing the moment.

If the list isn't quite your thing, practicing gratitude can happen in other ways. Instead of spending time to write out your personal list, try sharing gratitude daily with others in written or verbal forms. Plan to start each week or each day sending a note of appreciation to tell someone how they've made a difference in your life. Be specific about why you're thankful.

If you're thinking this all sounds a little too whimsical, research shows gratitude increases resilience, happiness, and self-awareness.[1] It also has been found to lead to physical health benefits, including better sleep.[2] Most of the studies showed significant positive effects of gratitude can be developed within three months. That's such a small part of your entire life, and yet the effects will extend far beyond three months. To grow in your career, these are all qualities you will need, so think of it as an investment in your professional success.

In cultivating gratitude in my daily life, I've grown more optimistic, resilient, and open to learning (and failure). It has helped me overcome challenges in handling change on many occasions. I've realized I had the tools I needed within myself. I've taught this to my son, to help him create this strength in himself, too, and it's become part of our dinner conversations or bedtime routines.

When you feel grateful, you honor all you have and all you are.

AND MINDSET

Here's the thing: You can be grateful and ambitious. These are two equally important truths, and they don't have to exist independently. A paradox mindset means accepting the both/and of the situation[3]—meaning multiple things can be true at the same time. This is the reality of life: things may feel competing or in tension, but you can reframe your approach to see how they integrate. It's what I call the *And* Mindset.

The sooner you accept this paradox, the sooner you'll thrive. In the *And* Mindset, you see abundance. You believe in possibility—including what's possible for you. There's space for all of us to be successful, there's space for all feelings, and in this magical space, there's innovation, grace, and learning.

When you're stressed or overwhelmed, it's a natural response to see everything as zero sum. There's only one option. There's only one winner. There's only one path forward. People crave clarity and certainty, and we unintentionally try to create it such that it overshadows other important truths. You can get caught up in either/ or—and it will limit you.

Honor the tension that exists when two competing things feel true.

You can find joy even in challenge.

You can love something and still be exhausted from it.

You can walk into the discomfort to get comfortable.

You can create clarity while you wade through ambiguity.

You have the power and strength to do this. It may need to be further cultivated, and I'm here to support you.

Find the *and*.

While you seek it, remember this is a process.

HAPPINESS MINDSET

Sometimes while you pursue goals, it's easy to get caught up in the results. You tell yourself: if I just do a little more, go a little farther, work a little harder, I'll reach the desired outcome. In this hustle, you might even lose sight of what you're working toward. I know I have.

This goes all the way back to childhood for me. I can distinctly remember conversations with my mother where I'd plot the next student leader role I wanted or a project I should take on, even when my days were already packed with a full roster of activities. I often looked ahead, working toward the next big thing. Though my mother always made sure to remind me that she was proud of me, in each conversation she would add, "Remember to have fun." I tried to take her words to heart, though usually I waited to celebrate until after the task was finished or the goal was completed. It wasn't lost on me that most of my friends' parents urged them to achieve, and mine told me to have fun. I think she realized she didn't need to push me because I pushed myself hard enough. Looking back, I remember far less about the goals I planned—which seemed so important to me at the time—than her gentle encouragement. She had already learned happiness doesn't come from reaching a goal. To my mom, joy came from celebrating the moment you were in.

This hustle continued as I entered the working world. I was motivated to exceed every goal, whether to prove to others or myself that I could. It felt great to make something happen as a result of my efforts and be recognized for it, which felt even better. This was how I defined success, and therefore happiness. The cycle continued—except it didn't always. When I didn't meet my goals, it gutted me. And sometimes even when I did meet them, I didn't acknowledge what I had accomplished because I was too busy working toward the next goal. I kept racing to the proverbial top of the mountain thinking that's where I would find happiness. But the problem was when I got there, I sometimes found that what I thought was the top was really only the middle of that mountain. Never mind the fact that I thought there were always more mountains to climb. Living like this meant being in a perpetual state of "not enough."

Getting out of this trap is crucial to your success, not to mention your emotional and personal well-being. If this feels like something you do, start to make a change by stopping yourself from equating reaching your goals to happiness.

Think about this. Do you tell yourself, "After I reach that goal, then I'll be happy"? If you do, there are some hard truths you need to come to accept. First, your goals may change. You also won't always meet them. You're more than your outcomes. And when you make happiness contingent on your success, you're inadvertently postponing your own joy. You deserve to be happy. Right. Now.

Happiness is a mindset. It comes from where you focus your attention and how you approach whatever your current reality is. I like to think of myself as a rational optimist, which means realistically assessing a situation and believing you can make a real difference. It's knowing that you can create clarity in ambiguity. I want to be clear this approach doesn't mean that you're naive or overly optimistic; instead, it means you can see challenges as possibilities.

PROGRESS MINDSET

Once you realize happiness leads to success and not the other way around, it doesn't necessarily mean you need to slow down in pursuing your goals. Instead, you'll have to be far more purposeful to give yourself pause in order to grow—and that's where our final mindset comes in: Progress Mindset.

Think about it: when you're so focused on your next accomplishment, you forget how hard you worked to get where you are. Before you move on to the next thing, first recognize your preparation and learning. The journey matters, and it's more meaningful when you recognize the steps you took. It's about believing in your own abilities, knowing you have the capacity to improve, and honoring what you did to get to this point.

Learning to celebrate progress has fundamentally shifted how I lead myself and others—and it's also become one of my greatest joys. Now I see every day as an opportunity to appreciate how far I've come—and it can be for you, too. I mean, who doesn't love a good celebration?

You can start by jotting down a note in your calendar each day about a win you had. By the end of the week, you'll have a list of wins. These tiny victories add up over time. You can also find ways to remind yourself of what you did to get to where you are today.

When I was a development intern in college, a mentor, Beth, brought me a plain manila folder that she called an "AttaGirl" folder. She said it was for keeping track of the notes and accolades I received, and I should look back through the folder on tough days. Though unsure why this would be important, I trusted her wisdom and dutifully took the folder, and this practice has become incredibly important to me as I've progressed throughout my career.

Over time, I've created email and paper versions of this folder. They are filled with my formal offer letter for my first job in fundraising, the envelope from the first seven-figure charitable gift I closed, notes from bosses recognizing my efforts, and cards from colleagues cheering me on, among other things.

On the days you make a mistake or get rejected, it's easy to forget the many things you have accomplished and how you have helped others. The simple act of reviewing the folder and rereading the notes provides you with the reinforcement to keep going, try again, learn from the experience, and refocus on the big picture. Today, it just takes *knowing* that the folder exists to motivate me. When I packed up my office during the pandemic to transition to fully remote work, it was one of my most prized office possessions.

Even when you've developed strategies to work through things over time, you'll likely still have moments where former tendencies emerge. There have been a few (okay, more than a few) times in adulthood where my mom still had to lightly remind me to have fun and be in the moment. Because you're committed to the journey, you can accept this learning with self-compassion.

MY MOMENT OF REALIZATION

When I think back through the rejections I received throughout my career, one in particular has stayed with me all these years. I had my eye on a job managing young alumni fundraising for a university I had strong affinity for (though I hadn't attended). As a recent graduate who was passionate about helping others find the joy in philanthropy, I felt this was the perfect job for me. I made it to the final interview round, and ultimately, they selected someone else. I remember feeling brokenhearted that this had been my chance, and I missed it. Then I learned the woman who got the job (I'll call her Laura) had several years of experience already, she was an alumna, and on top of all that, she seemed to have it all together. While Laura seemed perfect for the job (and really, in life), I felt less great about myself.

Even after I found a job and moved away, I still randomly thought about how I had missed the perfect opportunity and Laura had gotten it. It's a little embarrassing to admit, but I would follow her career and secretly compare our progress against each other, too.

Imagine my surprise when I went to a professional development conference a few years later and saw Laura's name on the attendee list. During a break, I worked up the courage to introduce myself. I wanted to dislike her, to confirm she didn't have real experience and I really should have been the one to get the job all those years ago, but in reality, Laura was well spoken, knowledgeable about our industry, and kind. Instead of hating her, *I wanted to be her*. I invited Laura to join a group of us for lunch and felt a little starstruck. At the end of the conference, we exchanged business cards and said we'd keep in touch.

We talked on the phone a few times and ran into each other once shortly after. The magic of the internet allowed me to continue to follow Laura's successes, and there were many. She continually received promotions and took on new roles. Even though I was on a similar trajectory, it didn't seem to move as smoothly or quickly as it did for her. The moves we made for my husband's career often required me to take a lateral opportunity. I daydreamed about whether my career might look like Laura's if I had the chance to make my own decisions.

Over time, though, I stopped checking in quite as often on what Laura was up to. My own career and life began to fulfill me in a different way. In addition to the professional roles I loved, I had started writing more on my blog, and one day I noticed a comment from Laura on a post I had shared. I sent her a brief note to thank her for writing and said how meaningful it was, especially from someone whose career I had followed from the beginning. She responded with a note of her own, "You have helped me SO much this year!! Last week I accepted my dream job. . . . So proud of who you are, where you are, and what you are doing. You are the example!"

I burst into tears when I read it. I had spent nearly 20 years of my life proving why I should have gotten that job, and in some ways, wanting to be this woman who thought *I am the example.*

I share this story with you because I want to help you learn an invaluable lesson it took me too long to realize: you need to stop proving yourself to everyone and shift your mindset. Start cheering yourself on, finding gratitude, creating happiness, and celebrating your progress. You're inspiring others, sometimes in ways you'll never know.

It's time to get out there. And it's time to start making your one Bold Move a day.

BOLD MOVES TO MAKE NOW

Look back over the four mindsets. Which one will you try first this week? How will you get started?

Write down one of your wins from this week in your calendar or phone.

Create an "AttaGirl" folder for yourself (either a paper or email version—or both!) and find two things to add to it.

Believe in Yourself

Believing in yourself is the foundation for how you will do everything in your work and life. Throughout your career, there will be people who try to undermine your confidence (knowingly or unknowingly), so it's important to be clear about what makes you great, how to keep moving forward through challenges, and why you belong at any table.

Learning how to believe in yourself will be a lifelong process. As I've entered each new stage in my career, I've felt unsure of myself. Whether you're starting your first job, are starting a new role at a new organization, have recently been promoted, or are returning to work from parental or any other kind of leave, it's normal to feel uncertain as you navigate through something for the first time. This is also where your greatest growth opportunities will be.

Though you may be starting something new, it doesn't take away all the things you've worked toward to get to this point. But it does mean you have to consider how to leverage all your experiences to bring the best of yourself to the situation.

In one of my first jobs as a development director at a university, though I had worked hard to get to where I was, I felt like I had to prove to everyone I deserved to be there. I also felt the need to prove it to myself. I held myself to unrealistic standards. For example, instead of recognizing this time as an opportunity to learn, I stayed late at the office working on projects, revising them multiple times, and sometimes even brought myself to tears in frustration when my work didn't turn out right.

I learned the hard way in this job that when you focus on doing everything "right," it undermines your confidence because things don't (and won't) always go as planned. I also learned that I needed to start asking for help. At the time, I didn't think that was an option, because I was worried my supervisor and colleagues would think I wasn't good enough or didn't know enough. I didn't want them to think I was a fraud for having this job, because deep down I felt like I was. Looking back, this was probably the time in my life when my self-doubt was at its worst.

Fortunately, I had a supportive boss, Pam, who provided guidance about how things were done while giving me a safe space to develop new ideas. She delegated important tasks to me and always took the time to thoroughly explain her expectations.

But she wasn't going to figure it all out for me. I had to do the work, too.

After one particularly challenging situation with a colleague, I went to her to say I couldn't work with that person anymore. I drew a line in the sand and expected her to fix it. Not only did she refuse to do that, but she also lectured me on what my job really was—to learn how to navigate things for myself and collaborate with others in order to succeed. I remember leaving her office and crying in the parking lot for a long time. I wish I could say I walked into the office the next day truly understanding the importance of that feedback, but I didn't. Though I felt defeated, something did become clear: it would be up to me to lead myself and improve this situation, and that's what I would do.

Even when you're at the top of your career, you'll still have to remember to do this. I know I did. As I navigated the challenges of being a senior VP, I made some missteps. When I first started, I relied too heavily on what had worked for me in the past and didn't recognize that things were different in a new role and organization. If I had focused more on learning how to integrate the expectations of this new organization with my strengths, I would have brought my best self to work much sooner. During times like this when the little voice in your head tells you you're not good enough, consider this: if you listen closely enough, there can also be another even stronger voice reminding you that *this* is exactly what you were made for. In those moments, which voice you listen to is your choice. You have the choice to be your own biggest fan. Because if you want others to believe in you, you'll have to believe in yourself first. And believing in yourself doesn't mean you have everything figured out; it means taking on a challenge anyway. Confidence is taking action to move you closer to your potential.

CREATE A STRONG FOUNDATION

Whether you're in your first job, a first-time manager, or leading a company, remember you're in your role for a reason. They hired you because they saw the strengths you could bring to the role. It's important for you to see these strengths and reflect on what makes you distinctly special.

Whitney Johnson, author of *Disrupt Yourself*, calls the unique gifts that make you who you are your superpowers. I love the idea of having superpowers, just by being yourself!

Let's spend some time reflecting on what sets you apart. This is not a time to self-edit; it's a time to get to know yourself better. Whether you're a journal person or not, what follows is an excellent way to help yourself answer this question.

Here are some prompts to determine your superpowers:[1]

1. What compliments do you hear frequently?
2. What do your friends ask you for advice about?
3. What comes naturally to you that doesn't come naturally to others?

Here, as an example, are my answers to the prompts:

1. **What compliments do you hear frequently?** I love connecting with super ambitious women who are at the top of their careers. I'm struck in nearly every networking conversation that people will thank me for truly listening to them and helping them think through complex situations they don't often talk about, even with people they know well. At first, I shrugged this off, because I was being myself and genuinely wanting to understand another woman's motivations and dreams. As I heard it again and again, I realized there was something here to explore—how few spaces there are for ambitious women to share their stories—and that's part of what prompted me to intentionally create this space through this community.

2. **What do your friends ask you for advice about?** Friends often come to me to talk through challenging conversations at work: how to ask for a promotion or negotiate their salary, what to do with a difficult boss or colleague, or how to advocate for themselves. When your friends come to you for guidance on a specific topic, that's a signal they see you as an expert from their perspective.

16

3. **What comes naturally to you that doesn't come naturally to others?** I happen to have an excellent memory, which enables me to recall conversations, situations, or policies that others may forget or need notes for. To be clear, this is both a superpower and kryptonite, because I don't necessarily want to remember all these details—and other people don't necessarily want me to either! For example, I get frustrated when we talk about the same topics over and over in meetings, especially when we don't move toward action. And my loving husband wishes I would not mentally track who did what.

I love doing this superpower exercise at different points in my life and career, because it really helps you understand how you can bring value where you are and what to do more of depending on your current situation. When you fully leverage your strengths, you bring goodness to the world—and more joy for you.

If you're thinking right now, "I have absolutely no idea what my unique qualities are," that's a sign to dig deeper and get curious. Here's the thing: these strengths come so naturally to you, you may not even notice them, unless you slow down to pay attention.

Maybe you have the ability to inspire others around a common cause, or you see what others overlook, or you thoughtfully analyze data to make recommendations. For more inspiration, go back through your "AttaGirl" folder and review what others have sent to you celebrating your great work.

Once you have clarified what your strengths are, feel confident in your abilities, and value what you bring to the world, you'll start believing others when they start to recognize them, too. Learning how to graciously accept compliments when others acknowledge what you've done well builds your confidence and has the power to deepen relationships with others.

Let's practice:

Colleague: "You killed it in the presentation today."

You: "*Thank you.*"

That's it.

It's about time we all remember that "Thank you" is a full sentence.

Don't deflect the praise because it feels awkward to get attention or you're focused on the one thing you could have done better in the presentation. Don't minimize your work because you think things like that are "just doing your job," either. Instead, say "Thank you" and mean it. Recognize your own awesomeness, and be grateful that someone else saw it, too. You'll help other women around you see how they can simply accept a compliment themselves, too!

Learning how to accept a compliment gave me freedom to celebrate what makes me special, and that was one of the greatest gifts I have learned and earned. And speaking of gifts, want to know another one? *You don't need anyone else to validate your amazingness.* Don't get me wrong, I will happily accept genuine recognition, and I do find that it motivates me. But learning to compliment *myself* gave me the power to believe in myself and be my best self.

And I want that for you, too.

OVERCOME YOUR OWN LIMITING BELIEFS

Even after you've created your strong foundation and start to truly believe in yourself, you will experience moments of uncertainty and doubting your own abilities. These feelings, though uncomfortable, are common.

Limiting beliefs can creep up at any stage in your career and in unexpected moments, such as the high points of your career. This happened to me shortly after I got a big promotion at work and headed to New York for an important donor visit, something I had done hundreds of times before. Except this time, I experienced a gnawing feeling that maybe I didn't really know what I was doing and wasn't ready after at all. I ignored it while navigating the train and subway to the meeting, focusing instead on how I wanted the conversation to go. Everything was relatively fine until the elevator ride up to the office's fancy coffee bar, where I felt dizzy, and the negative voice grew louder in my head.

I had only a few moments before the bank partner would expect to meet me for coffee. Looking frantically around the lobby, I found a ladies' room because I needed to quiet my mind. I recalled moments as a kid when I would feel unsure of myself or broken from rejection, and my mother would stand beside me and lift me back up by encouraging me to build my own self-worth. She would gently guide me to a nearby mirror and encourage me to look at my own reflection to remind myself I was worthy and deserved good things.

While I watched my own reflection in the expansive mirror, I grounded myself by repeating silently my new title and organization. Over and over, I said, "I am the director of major gifts at the Wharton School." To be clear, I don't encourage you to wrap yourself up so tightly in your title as the indicator of your worthiness, because you are so much more than your job. But in that moment, I needed to remind myself I had earned that role and I belonged where I was. Slowly I felt the negative voice get quieter. I walked into the meeting room and asked for one of the largest gifts I had ever asked for in my career—and I did so because I was the right person for the job and I was damn good at it, too.

There's incredible power in having a mantra to rely on and help you refocus when you're feeling overwhelmed or lost. It doesn't matter so much what the mantra is, it just matters that it reminds you how amazing you are and what you're capable of. Here's one to get you started: "I will achieve things I didn't know were possible." "I will make one Bold Move a day" is another great one!

After my meeting that day, I called my best friend to recount both the highs and lows of the trip. She responded with empathy and shared a story about a time she had questioned her own abilities in the midst of a complex work project she had worked hard to get. It was a reminder that when you face self-doubt, you're not alone. Share with a friend or mentor how you're feeling. They've likely gone through this, too, and can relate to your experiences.

This can even be something you add to your list of questions for when you meet people you admire: ask them about a time when they felt less sure of themselves and what they've done to overcome those moments. Learning from others will help you remember you're not alone and build your strategies to get back up again in the future.

Here's the thing: You did the work to get where you are, and you belong at the table. Things don't just happen to you. Luck is when preparation meets opportunity.

Make your one Bold Move a day. It is an excellent way to choose confidence and believe in yourself.

FACE YOUR FEARS

Once you've chosen to accept and embrace what makes you unique, the next step is to work through your fears—even while you're still learning and making mistakes. Common fears in work life can include failure, not being good enough, being wrong, and disappointing others. I know this because I've feared all of these at different points in my career: I've focused on what I was "supposed to do" so I could be deemed "good enough." I've gotten caught up in other people's expectations. And I've let my fear of failure stop me from starting.

The reality is you can't advance yourself and your career unless you're willing to face your fears. To be clear: I'm not saying you have to *overcome* your fear. I'm instead saying you have to learn how to do the things *while you feel afraid*, so the fear doesn't overwhelm you. This is where you level up.

You may try to ignore your feelings in the moment because it seems easier than dealing with them. But fighting or ignoring your feelings can lead to shame. While it may feel obvious to acknowledge you have fears, you have to first give yourself permission to feel them because this isn't something you'll find externally. Look within and ask yourself: What approval do I need from myself?

Asking this question creates self-awareness of your feelings. From there, you can get more specific about what you're worried about. Naming your feelings gives you power over them. Thinking through where these feelings have emerged in past situations helps you get started. You may even write down what you can recall from those experiences. (For example, "When I presented an idea in the meeting last time, I got shot down by the managing partner. I was mortified and I could see everyone looking at me. I didn't speak for the rest of the meeting.") Your goal is to understand where these worries come from because that will give you insights into what you need to do to work through them.

You may unintentionally get in your own way by staying focused on what's happened in the past, going all the way back to your childhood. I remember the feeling of politely sitting on the sidelines during games and activities as a kid, because I was too afraid to try something new. After all, new things are much harder to do perfectly, and I thought perfect was the only option. Because of this, I held myself back time and time again.

Here's the thing: I still hold myself back at times. I overthink things or wish I could avoid them altogether, until I remember all of this is a choice. Fears can hold you back—or you can channel your energy to use your fears to help you move forward. The very act of feeling fear reminds you to be present in the moment you're in.

We spend so much time picturing the worst-case scenarios. Good things are possible, maybe even the best things. Thinking about the best possible outcomes requires you to shift your mindset to consider why good things can happen to and for you. Expecting the best is more vulnerable than expecting the worst. Focusing on the worst-case outcome protects you from being disappointed when things don't work out. You might even convince yourself you knew something bad would happen, so you prevented yourself from considering other options. When you limit your thinking this way, you also limit what's possible for yourself. Ask yourself, "What's the best possible outcome that can happen?"

But know that things won't always be linear. You may feel comfortable asking for a raise, but not asking the server to fix your meal order. (Okay, that may just be me.)

Whatever it is that you struggle with, commit knowing that you're worth what you are dreaming of—even if it's as small as having mustard on the side of your meal like you asked for. Little things can be big things, and those little things can help you start somewhere.

Like most experiences, it takes practice to achieve a desired outcome, and one of the best ways to practice facing your fears is to make your one Bold Move every day. This builds your courage. It won't always turn out the way you've planned or hoped—but it just might turn out even better.

BUILD RESILIENCE

I personally and firmly believe anything is possible. I show up at work and for others each day and lead with optimism and a belief that people I care about can do things they didn't know were possible.

It's easy to presume that someone who appears to have boundless positive energy wouldn't get caught up in the little, everyday frustrations of work and life—or the big challenges we all face.

I'm going to let you in on a secret . . . I used to be a pessimist. If you know me now, that might really surprise you, but it's true. When people ask, "Do you see the glass half full or half empty?" I used to (almost proudly) shout, "Half empty!" I could find the negative side of everything, even in a positive moment. When I was happy—and I definitely was happy often—I worried about being *too* happy, as if the joy might run out or something bad was bound to happen next. Now I see that this all probably related to having anxiety that I wasn't willing to acknowledge or work on at the time.

Over time, I learned that the difference between a pessimist and an optimist is *how you approach whatever your reality is.* And once I realized that I was in control of my reality, everything changed. Even in the difficult moments, I stopped seeing barriers, and instead started to see opportunities.

Resilience means knowing how to rely on your inner strength and grow through your circumstances. It doesn't, however, mean you won't experience challenge.

In fact, I still feel rejection, frustration, lack of motivation, and disappointment (sometimes all in the same day!). But the difference now is that I get back up after that—and most times even more determined.

This is what I want for you, too. Here are four ways to build your resilience:

Focus on What You Can Control

When working through challenges, you may feel overwhelmed by your own worries. If this happens, a great place to get started is to write all of your thoughts down in a list. Consider each individual thought you're having, and ask yourself, "Can I control this?" (For the record, you cannot control the future, other people's actions or feelings, or outcomes, no matter how much you or I try). If you cannot control it, focus on what you *are* able to influence or change, including your mindset, effort, and actions. Resilience comes from focusing and protecting your energy.

After you've done that work, ask yourself "How can I best approach this situation right now?"

Change Your Perspective

One of the things you can control is your perspective. Though you cannot change what happened, you can choose how you respond. I once read about the importance of saying "I get to do this" (as opposed to "I have to . . ."). Though it's a small nuance in the language, the messages you send yourself affect how you think and feel. Create a sense of autonomy in whatever situation you're in by saying, "I choose this" or "I can change this." View challenge as an opportunity to learn or problem to be solved, rather than an insurmountable obstacle or barrier. Also believe that good things can happen even in the most difficult moments. (This is the *And* Mindset in practice!) When you reframe something negative in more positive terms, you can change how your brain perceives the challenge.[2]

Offer Compassion to Yourself

How kind are you . . . to yourself? We often think about offering compassion to others, but research shows being kind to *yourself* strengthens your resilience.[3] That's because when you allow yourself grace, you also create space to iterate, innovate, and get back up stronger.

Being self-compassionate means holding yourself account-able *and* feeling motivated to achieve. You already know that disappointment and failure are inevitable, so you're better prepared to face these difficult situations.

Lean on Your Loved Ones

Everyone experiences difficult moments in their careers and per-sonal lives—and you shouldn't have to face them alone. Asking for help is a sign of strength and resilience. Lean on the people you're close to, whether that's a colleague, family member, or friend. If you don't have those people in your life right now, count on me. I believe in you and what is possible for you, even if you have forgot-ten this for yourself for just a moment. When you let others in, you model for them that it's okay to do this for themselves, too. It will also give them a sense of purpose by being able to support you. If you're feeling particularly overwhelmed, you may consider reach-ing out to a medical professional. There is no gold medal for trying to figure everything out on your own. Community and connec-tion are at the core of being human, and we aren't meant to go at life alone.

Building resilience won't happen overnight; it takes time. And practicing the skills associated with bouncing back will help you navigate whatever challenges you face today or in the future—every single step is worth celebrating.

BOLD MOVES TO MAKE NOW

Ask yourself the question prompts on page 16 to identify at least three of your superpowers.

Practice saying "Thank you" to a compliment you receive.

Decide what your mantra(s) will be to keep you focused on your strengths.

Achieving Your Goals

At various times throughout your career, you may wonder if you're on the right path, doing enough to advance at work, or what your goals should be.

I'm a big fan of talking these kinds of questions through with a trusted mentor; however, I recognize that's not always an option. If that's the case for you, imagine that you're having coffee with me, and we are talking through all of this together right now.

Over time, I've learned the importance of developing goals for myself based on *who* I wanted to become, not just *what* I wanted to accomplish. And that distinction is what I want to help you to realize and live.

Achieving your goals requires intentional reflection and preparation—and that's what we'll be doing in this chapter through multiple exercises. A research study done at Dominican University in California showed that writing down your goals makes you 42 percent more likely to achieve them, so be sure to really put in the work and spend the time working through this chapter.[1] These steps are necessary and will set you up for success going forward.

CLARIFYING YOUR PURPOSE

You wake up every day and do your best at work and in life and then do it all again the next day. But what if you could create more clarity for yourself—and through this, you could also bring new energy to what you do? Thinking about *your purpose* may feel overwhelming, but it really means understanding what is most important to you and how to do more of the things that bring you joy.

The answers to these questions may not be immediately clear, so I've created a way to guide your reflection. I recommend designating time each day for a week to do this exercise (including weekends since your purpose extends beyond your job and career!). At the beginning or end of each day, spend a few minutes simply writing down your thoughts on a journal or note card. (You can combine this and your gratitude journal into one.) I'll get you started with a new writing prompt in each of the sections below.

Reflect on What's Important to You

Before anything else, I want to start by saying it's totally okay if you have not yet spent time reflecting on your priorities before today. That being said, I encourage you to spend some time doing this now. It's especially helpful to be clear on what's important to you when experiencing change at work or in life, and definitely before you make any changes of your own, such as starting a job search or moving to a new city.

Day 1 Writing Prompt: What are the nonnegotiable aspects of your life?

This is the start of clarifying what's important to you, how you're already activating these parts of your life, and what you want to further cultivate over time.

Remember Where You Started

Next, think about what you wanted to be when you grew up. Now try to remember *why* you wanted to be that. As a child, I dreamt of being a writer, social worker, rabbi, and even a fashion designer. For me, my career dreams were always about helping others (while rocking amazing clothes!), and one of my strengths is sharing a vision, through speaking or writing, to inspire others to achieve what they didn't think possible. What about you?

Day 2 Writing Prompt: What did you want to be when you were growing up? What about that profession motivated you?

Again, it's okay if your dream is far removed from what you're now doing. The point of this writing exercise is to see if you can connect your early interests to your present-day life—and how that might clarify what you want your life to look like in the future.

Pay Attention to Consistent Compliments

Think about what others say you do well. Like when your colleagues have told you how they can always rely on you for [insert impressive thing about you here]. Reflect on positive feedback your bosses have given to you. Keep in mind, your superpowers extend beyond work. When your friends tell you how much you amaze them, consider what strengths they're referring to.

Day 3 Writing Prompt: What compliments do you frequently receive? What themes run throughout this recognition?

You may unintentionally downplay these things because they come so naturally to you, these are the same superpowers we talked about in Chapter 2!

Focus on What You Like to Do

Think about your best days at the office and how you spend your time on those days. When you feel excited about your work, you work harder. (Except that same work often doesn't feel hard because it utilizes your inherent talent.)

All jobs will have tasks that aren't your favorite, but if you believe work should mean more than a paycheck, you absolutely deserve to look for work where you can find purpose and, hopefully, fun.

Day 4 Writing Prompt: What projects bring you energy? When do you feel most fulfilled at work? Write down the words you use to describe the ideal work culture for you.

Being clear on what joyful and meaningful work looks like for you can help you find a job more closely aligned with what will bring out the best in you.

Consider What You Admire About Others

Once at a conference I attended, participants were asked to share about their favorite bosses and why they were selected. It was a worthwhile reflection on what we value in our leaders. In sharing my story with the group, I realized I had internalized my former boss's traits that I admired so much and worked to demonstrate them in my own leadership each day. I also have colleagues, friends, and family members I admire and learn from, aspiring to follow their examples. Earlier in my career I even carried a notecard in my purse with each of these people's names and the character trait I admired most about them. It was a reminder both that they were with me in my daily life and of what I wanted to pursue in my own leadership.

Day 5 Writing Prompt: Write down a list of people you admire and what traits you admire about them.

Some people suggest these esteemed traits reflect your own strengths because you have to understand them to notice them in others.

Consider Your Why

Your why is your north star. I first read about this in Simon Sinek's book, *Start with Why*, which helped me to understand what matters most to me and how to articulate it to others. Your why isn't what you do or your job title. It's what motivates you and should translate across all areas that are important to you personally and professionally.

Here's the formula to develop and communicate your why: "My why is to [*Fill in this blank with your contributions, what you bring to the world*] so that [*Fill in this blank with your impact, how you use those contributions to positively affect others*]."[2]

Let me share my why with you, so you can see how it works: *My why is to help others achieve more than they thought possible, so that they can fulfill their potential and find joy.*

Day 6 Writing Prompt: What is your why?

When you focus on why you do things, you'll position yourself to live according to your values and thrive as a whole person. Your why is about what motivates you—and sharing it with others can help motivate them, too.

Find Your Joy

When I learned to develop the Gratitude Mindset, I started to find joy in unexpected places and ways. A favorite coffeeshop. The way the light comes through the trees at a certain time of day. Sending a seemingly random text to someone who responds that it was just what they needed at that moment. Orange shoes. You might resonate with some of the joys on my list, and you'll want to spend time identifying what joy looks and feels like to you. This is, after all, about *your best life.*

Day 7 Writing Prompt: What are some of your happiest moments? Where do you find joy?

Recalling your happiest moments might just make you feel happy all over again, which is an added benefit. Keep in mind that you have to proactively *recognize* moments of joy to feel them, so consider what you might do to remind yourself to acknowledge those moments.

When you complete all seven reflection prompts, you won't necessarily have full clarity on your purpose, but you will have taken meaningful action toward understanding yourself. This will serve as a perfect springboard to propel you forward.

SETTING GOALS FOR YOURSELF

In 2018, I began to invest more in my writing and set two huge goals that I wanted to accomplish one day. I call these unicorn goals: those super ambitious accomplishments you want to work for, even if you're the only one who believes they can be real. My unicorn goals were:

1. Write a book (yesssss!).
2. Write an article for *Harvard Business Review*.

I kept these goals mostly to myself at first, but I eventually revealed them to my new writing coach, Sara. At the time, I had barely any bylines to my name. I had only recently started writing consistently. To her credit, she didn't laugh or say, "Shanna, that's never going to happen." She said, "Okay, well, where are you going to start right now?"

That's my advice to you right now. Ask yourself that same question: "Where are you going to start with your goals?"

In 2019, I started writing with the intention of submitting to book agents. I wrote early mornings, weekends, and vacations. By the end of the year, I had 40,000 words, which would eventually become the beginning of a first draft of a book. I spent the week between Christmas and New Year's preparing my book submission materials and cover letters to agents. At the beginning of 2020, I sent out 30 queries and excitedly waited for responses.

Only then did I practice sharing my goals (out loud—eek!) with friends and in networking conversations. It was a big deal for me to share what I was working toward knowing it might not happen—knowing I might fail. But realized willingness to ask for help connected me more deeply with others, too. In the end, being vulnerable helped me get closer to my goals, and it built more meaningful relationships.

Now that people knew about my unicorn goals, an author friend connected me to her agent. I traveled to New York City for us to meet, and from the moment I walked in the door, I could feel I was being evaluated by her. She repeatedly asked me about my book vision, audience, and what was different about my project—and I left knowing that she didn't think I answered her questions in my writing or in our conversation. I walked the long way back to the train station so I could process this all more fully and slowly realized I was much farther away from my goal than I wanted to be.

Over the next few months, each book query I sent was rejected. With the first few, I was disappointed, but hopeful. As more came in, I felt heartbroken and uncertain. By the beginning of March, when nearly all of them had responded "no, thank you," I was devastated.

I remember one morning in particular, when I broke down crying after I had dropped my son off at school. My husband was on an international business trip, so I was home alone. I realized I could mourn the loss by myself, or I could reach out for support. I turned to a group of women I had met through a working mother's professional network whom I had grown very close to. Each of them responded to me with compassion and encouragement, as well as practical suggestions. Though I was no closer to reaching my goal, I felt much less alone.

As my book goal was paused by the universe (and the entire universe was paused due to the Covid-19 pandemic), I turned my attention toward my other unicorn goal: writing for *Harvard Business Review.*

HBR was the trusted resource I had relied on throughout my career, so it felt meaningful to be able to contribute my writing to this publication to help others. By then, I had practiced strengthening my writing and had experienced both rejection and acceptance at various publications. When I finally worked up my nerve to submit to *HBR*, I got rejected. Twice. But I kept trying, and with the next submission I finally got accepted. Today, I've published not just one, but multiple articles on *HBR* and made my second unicorn goal a reality.

And I bet you're wondering how this connects to my first unicorn goal, the one you know I achieved because you're holding this book. Well, that goal came to be in part because of my hard work making those *HBR* articles happen. Without achieving one goal and experiencing the hardships I dealt with along the way, this book wouldn't exist.

Develop Your Goals

Are you finally feeling ready to set some goals of your own? If so, here are some questions for you to keep that process moving:

What do you want to learn? The goal should be more than your desired outcome. Aim for new learning, which is possible whether or not you reach the goal.

How long will it take you? Try to estimate a realistic timeline to work toward this goal, understanding that humans tend to have a planning fallacy.[3] You may need to add 15 to 25 percent more time as a buffer.

What will success look like for you? Be specific about what success looks (and feels) like, so you know what it is when you get there. It will be worthwhile to have several success markers along the way so you can celebrate progress.

Why is this important to you? If a goal is not important to you or for someone else, it will be challenging to motivate yourself. Be clear on what's important about your goal, even if it's a tangential reason.

How does this get you closer to who you want to become?
Create unicorn goals for yourself, because you know in your heart you are meant for something bigger.

While these questions serve as a good place to start, you'll have to dig deeper by answering tougher questions, too. Here are a few to get you started:

What (if any) sacrifices are you willing to make to reach your goal? Achieving a big goal will likely require you to give up something else that is important to you. You'll also have to keep working toward your goal, even when others try to redirect you (intentionally or unintentionally).

Who will support you as you work toward your goals? Your circle should be full of the kind of people who remind you that you were brave enough to set bold goals, no matter what the outcome.

Are you prepared for the journey, or do you only hope for the outcome? Wanting the outcome won't be enough to sustain you in the most challenging moments.

What systems will you put into place to achieve your goal? (More on this next.)

Create a System to Achieve Your Goals

A goal gives you direction, but a system is what helps you actually make forward progress. With this in mind, if you want to achieve the goals you've set for yourself, you'll need to build a system to set yourself up for success. The more structure and intentionality, the more likely you'll be to follow through.

You can level up this system even more through defining when, how, and with whom you'll work toward your goals.

Structure Your Goals

If you want to achieve your goals, you must figure out what micro-steps you need to take now to get there. Want to write a book? Start with writing 1,000 words every day. Maybe you'd like to create your own business? Start with 30 minutes of learning each day. While those steps might seem too small, it's best to start out with tiny steps to build a habit that can one day get you to reach your unicorn goal.

One way to make sure those habits stick is to create cues that connect behaviors. James Clear, author of *Atomic Habits*, calls this "habit stacking."[4]

It looks like this:

- After I brush my teeth, I'll do 10 push-ups.
- After I make my tea, I'll sit down to write.
- Before I serve breakfast to my family, I'll exercise.

By connecting new habits to a system that already exists in your life, you'll find integrating these habits to be much more seamless than you anticipated.

If you want to be even more sure your habits stick, name drop to yourself when you set your goals. Research shows saying "you" or your name makes you more likely to perform better, especially under stress.[5] Using the tea example from above, you would shift the language to say:

- After Shanna makes her tea, she'll sit down to write.
- After you make your tea, sit down to write.

The most important thing is to show up consistently for yourself, to demonstrate to yourself that you can do this, and create a system that gets you started in the right direction.

Partner with Others on Your Goals

Many years ago, one of my dearest friends and I were working toward promotions at the same time. It was a topic that came up often in our phone conversations. At some point during our call, we had the idea to become formal accountability partners. We created parameters for the partnership: We would have specifically designated calls for these conversations. We would each define a goal we wanted to work on and report on our progress. We also agreed we would read the same book that related to what we were each trying to accomplish and share our takeaways.

Because my accountability partner was a close friend, it allowed me to be vulnerable about my successes and mistakes, and this is beneficial when it comes to this kind of partnership—but you don't have to be best friends for this to work well. Have you ever thought of having an accountability partner?

In one of my favorite research studies, a hill appears 20 percent steeper when you're by yourself than when you're with other people.[6] Whether your hill is literal or figurative, find someone who can help motivate and encourage you to achieve your goals. The only requirement is that the person is committed to your success and their own.

Here's how to get started:

1. Identify someone who could be your accountability partner. Ideally, it's someone who is in a similar place in life to you. This person isn't a mentor in a traditional sense but is a peer mentor.
2. Talk through how you want to structure check-ins.
3. Be specific about what your goal is.
4. Follow through on your check-in process and support each other.
5. Adjust or revise goals as needed.

You're far more likely to achieve your goals when you have someone keeping track with you on a consistent basis—and most important, cheering you on.

Be Flexible with Your Goals

One final note about your goals: give yourself grace while you hold yourself accountable to your big dreams. So much of what we talk about with making Bold Moves is preparing for what happens when things don't go as planned. This matters in goal setting, too, because you're human. There will be days where you're feeling too tired or stressed. Research shows you'll have a higher likelihood of attaining your goal if you plan ahead that you may trip up once or twice; however, you should consider those misses to be exceptions.[7] These same studies show that just knowing this is built into your plan could motivate you to "get back to work on a long-term goal after [you] fail at reaching an interim goal that is part of the process." Instead of giving up or being demotivated, you'll be more self-compassionate, because you anticipated an off day might happen.

PROGRESS > PRODUCTIVITY

As you already know, the Progress Mindset is an essential part of the formula for one Bold Move a day because it reminds you to celebrate how far you've come, both personally and professionally. You may mistake your accomplishments for "what you've completed," but you are more than your outcomes—and that's where the idea of productivity complicates things.

Productivity often refers to checking things off your list. It measures how efficient you are and is based on your output volume. However, this misses the point that productivity doesn't necessarily relate to work that is the best and highest use of your time. Plus, there will always be a never-ending list of things you can do. That's why *progress is far more important when it comes to goals and true success.*

Progress is how you're actually able to move something forward. It's working toward the biggest goals and projects and honoring each step of the process that gets you there. It's recognizing the wins and losses—and learning from both along the way.

Let's consider progress in the context of your work and career. Research shows progress is one of the biggest factors in how you feel about your job.[8] You feel more useful when you advance something that is important to you. This has a direct result on your motivation. On the other hand, you may be productive by checking things off of your to-do list each day, but if those tasks aren't moving you or your work in a direction that's meaningful to you, it's just busywork. This is why conflating progress and productivity at work and believing that your to-do list is a measure of success can result in keeping you exactly where you are.

So many people believe that being productive is what makes a day a success, yet when you rely on the sense of accomplishment that comes from a to-do list, you miss the value of recognizing what it took to get there. Think about it this way: if you checked off "signed a contract" on your to-do list, that might be satisfying, but wouldn't it be even more satisfying to recognize each and every step it took to make that accomplishment possible?

We need to enjoy the journey as much as the end result, and celebrating progress does exactly that. By shifting your focus from productivity to progress, you will begin to advance your work in a more meaningful way *and* honor how far you've come.

If you're a people leader, consider the role you play in creating a work environment in which it is possible for your team members to make progress in meaningful work. What barriers can you remove?

How are you connecting your team's projects to the broader organizational priorities? Research shows that helping employees make forward progress results in increased creativity and innovation, further reinforcing the importance of forward progress in supporting your team members and strengthening the organization at the same time.[9] Focusing on progress is a mindset shift, and it takes practice. Here are a few ways to recognize progress for yourself and encourage others to do the same:

1. Jot down in a journal or in the margin of your calendar what you were able to make progress on at the end of each day. We often forget to recognize what progress is, but this small act of writing down your progress each day will allow you to be more attuned to all the little things that move you forward—and reminds you to celebrate along the way.

2. Start your next team meeting asking everyone to share what they made progress on over the last week. The memory recall will reinforce the positive feelings, as will sharing it with others.

3. Go back through your "Atta Girl" folder. You'll be reminded of great things you've accomplished throughout your career and life, and most important, you'll see how far you've come.

4. In my office, I used to have a break-in-case-of-emergency bag of Trolli® sour gummy worms. When things felt overwhelming at work, they were my reward to stay motivated. Whether it's a sweet treat, booking a pedicure, or watching a show, create a way to celebrate yourself.

When you become more accustomed to honoring progress for yourself and others, you'll get an unexpected benefit—moving closer to your purpose. Purpose doesn't come from finishing the work—it comes from starting and moving forward.

WRITE A LETTER TO YOURSELF

Now that you've reflected on your purpose, considered your future goals, and developed a mindset and systems to help achieve them, it's time to formalize your intentions—and you can do this by writing a letter to yourself. Writing a letter to yourself is an opportunity to honor how far you've come while also staying focused on who you want to become. This letter is meant to be read only by you to celebrate your progress, recognize your strengths, and develop goals for your future growth. I do this each year and have kept all of these letters in a file to look back on.

These letters document my career journey and are snapshots of my life. Reading them gives me opportunities to celebrate progress on what I've achieved and reflect on what I've learned. Over time, I saw how my goals have changed—and how I have changed.

You can do this activity with your team, too. At the beginning of each fiscal year, I set aside time during a team meeting for everyone to write these letters. Team members were not expected to share their letters with anyone else, and yet there was a collective accountability to each other to know we were investing in ourselves together. Then they sealed the letters in envelopes, and I held them in a locked cabinet until the end of the year when we would open them at the same time to read individually.

Your letter can take on any format you choose. Here are some prompts to get you started:

1. What are three accomplishments you're proud of from the past year?
2. What is something you've been working on where you can celebrate progress?
3. What are three things you're grateful for from this year?
4. When did you feel at your best this year? How can you incorporate more of this into your daily routine?

5. What three goals (ideally a mix of personal and professional) do you want to work toward this year?

6. What will be your Boldest Moves over the next year? How will you incorporate making one Bold Move a day to achieve your goals?

You may decide to seal your letter in an envelope or keep it open on your desk or closet mirror. Either way, set a reminder for 12 months from now to revisit what you wrote.

The purpose of the letter is to celebrate how far you've come and remain true to your future aspirations. By documenting what's most important to you and using it to guide you, you set yourself up to advance your career and achieve your goals.

BOLD MOVES TO MAKE NOW

Write a letter to yourself using the prompts outlined in this chapter. Then set a calendar reminder to open it one year from now.

Decide one of your unicorn goals.

Identify a friend or colleague who can be an accountability partner for you.

Advance Your Career

Though my adult career has been focused and intentional, when I was younger, like most children I dreamed of many different careers (including a fashion designer, a social worker, a writer, and even a rabbi). Then at age 18, I found fundraising.

When I was a freshman in college, I came across a flyer advertising $10 per hour to stuff envelopes for the school's development office. I didn't know what development was, but as a kid I stuffed envelopes in my dad's office and he paid me $0.05 an envelope, so this was a serious upgrade.

When I showed up to work, there was a group of people around a long table with stacks of cards, envelopes, and stamps. From the conversation at the table, I learned the envelopes were invitations to one of the college's significant fundraising events, and I was asked if I wanted to serve as student worker for the event. I happily obliged.

On the night of the event, students stood in hallways and lobbies to direct guests to the gymnasium. After all of the guests settled, students were free to go, but I was invited to stay and stand in the back, if I liked. I stuck around and listened while a young man from a very wealthy family offered remarks about his beloved mentor.

This night ended up changing my life. I know this may sound a little magical, but it's my career origin story, and it's an important one to share. That night, I remember looking around the room and feeling I knew I was meant to be there. The people and remarks in the room seemed to move slowly while something quickly became clear to me: I was meant to be a fundraiser. Some people call this fate. Elizabeth Gilbert calls this a "Big Magic" moment.

Shortly after the event that night, I signed up to work in the regional development office. There, I was offered opportunities to learn alongside the other women in the office and manage projects. Their confidence in me bolstered how I felt about this future career choice—and myself. It also reinforced that I was ready for more learning and change on a bigger stage.

That desire for something bigger set me on a mission, and at 19, I cold-called Bob, the then–associate vice president of development at Duke University, to ask if he was hiring any development summer interns. He said no, and I asked him to consider hiring me anyway. A few weeks after that, I traveled to North Carolina to convince Bob to hire me for the summer, and he hired me back again the next summer, too. Those experiences set me on my path to my career in development today, and Bob remains one of my most treasured mentors all these years later.

As my time in college came to an end, I spent most of my senior year sending over 100 applications around the country to be a major gifts officer at a university. Numerous institutions brought me in for lengthy interviews all around the country before they rejected me with the explanation that I didn't have the experience needed for the role. In the end, not one university offered me a job.

I considered all the other things I enjoyed and could be good at and found a job that matched those criteria: a salesperson role at a women's retail company. All the while, I focused on cultivating my relevant skills so I'd be ready for a future fundraising role.

Eventually, through networking, I found a wonderful job raising money for a startup independent school that provided tuition-free education to middle school boys. At the same time, I was engaged and planning my wedding, and after just over a year on the job, my soon-to-be-husband received an offer for the doctoral program in pediatric psychology at the University of Alabama, one of the top programs for his area of study. We got married shortly after and two weeks later uprooted our lives for him to pursue his dream career.

Our first married home together was a rented apartment, and I was eager to get to work. Though I was committed to starting my career in higher education fundraising, there was a hiring freeze for employees at state institutions at the time, so I was without a job again, this time in an area where we knew no one. As hard as it had been not to get a job right after college, this unemployment period was psychologically harder for me. I had done everything to prepare, I had networked across my industry, and now I had experience.

I took a series of temporary positions to pay the bills. In the evenings, I attended networking events and joined a few community organizations to meet other people. Some days I doubted myself, and other days it was hard to leave the house. I cried a lot during this time, but I kept going.

I share all of this because I want you to know even when you are clear on what you want to do with your career, it will not necessarily be a clear path for you every step of the way. Each part of my story shows important pieces and moments when it comes to advancing your career—from networking, cultivating advisors and advocates, considering what's most important in a new role (or a new industry), and for some, all the way to pursuing entrepreneurship.

Let's dive deeper into each of those together now.

NETWORKING

You already know the benefits of networking to your career, yet you may still be reluctant to put yourself in those situations. I know that it feels uncomfortable to many people because reaching out when you want something, be it a new job or great advice, can feel disingenuous or self-serving. And it's not always easy to walk up to someone you don't know at a cocktail networking reception where awkward conversations about the weather (at worst) or what your job is (at best) seem to be the only things people talk about.

Here's a secret: as much as I love meeting new people, I wasn't always a fan of networking events. I've done the ballroom circle many times. I've also stood uncomfortably by a group of a few people where I tried to get into the conversation and still wasn't included. And I've definitely left cocktail hour shortly after using my free drink ticket at the bar.

But that's no longer the case. This is how I shifted my mindset.

First, imagine how you'd advise a friend in this situation. You would absolutely encourage your best friend to make connections, wouldn't you? You'd remind her that she's putting in a ton of hard work in contacting people, thoughtfully preparing for the meeting, and following up—and she doesn't need to feel like she's asking for special treatment.

Aren't you worth this investment too? You deserve to invest in your success.

Second, reframe what networking means. Change how you think about networking from "What can I get from others?" to "What can I give to others?" Once you do this, you'll find more comfort and greater success in your interactions, whether at an industry conference or an informational interview. Let's look at a few ways you can implement this in your next networking conversation.

Listen with Purpose

No matter who you're speaking to, there's something to learn from every interaction. This means whether you're in a conversation at a conference break, coffee shop, or informational interview, actively listen and ask thoughtful follow-up questions that build on what the other person says. To help make the conversation productive and enjoyable, listen with purpose. Ask yourself, "What can I learn from this?"

I've found that people are often willing to meet to share their personal story and, as a result, I learned from the best and simultaneously developed a deep network of industry leaders.

Offer Help

When you have the mindset to serve others while networking, you shift to building a genuine connection with someone. Plus, it takes the focus off of you. My favorite question to ask is, "What can I do to support your big goals for this year?" It's rewarding to champion people to achieve their dreams. Don't underestimate your ability to be helpful, even to someone more senior than you. You may be able to offer specialized skills or connect them to someone in your own network. And even if you can't directly influence outcomes, you can be supportive just by listening to the other person.

In time, you might even find yourself looking forward to networking events. And there's a bonus: when you put all this goodness into the world, it comes back to you in the future.

Schedule Your Time

Like any other professional skill, networking takes practice and effort. Strategically schedule time on your calendar for your networking activities and make them a priority. You may decide to request a meeting with someone new once a month or attend a professional association event once a quarter. Whatever you decide, commit to something that feels manageable and intentional, while also still stretching yourself a bit. Growth doesn't come without effort.

Make a Connection

When you reach out to someone to get coffee or lunch, I recommend you send a brief email that includes something of mutual interest. If you have a friend or acquaintance in common, share that (just make sure you check with these people before dropping their name!). You can even include what you admire about the person's career or what you would like to learn from them. If you're not able to meet at their office, you can offer Zoom or a phone call. Ask for only 20 minutes to show you respect the person's time. You can use the following template as a starting point.

> Dear X,
>
> I enjoyed [*hearing you speak/reading your article/ following your leadership to our profession/other connection point*]. I'd welcome learning more about your career. Would you be willing to speak with me for 20 minutes about how you got to where you are today? I'm happy to work around your schedule. [*Insert a talking point, such as something you two have in common or how you might be able to add value to them.*] Thank you for your consideration.
>
> Most sincerely,
> You

Ask for Advice (Not Favors)

Prepare in advance for networking conversations whenever you can. This is your chance to ask for advice, as well as learn about the person's career and experiences. Whether you're considering changing industries, seeking advancement in your field, or navigating a job search, you can tailor your questions to help support what you're looking to learn from the conversation.

Here are some sample questions you can use in networking conversations:

1. What led you to the career you have today?
2. What has been one of your most meaningful career experiences?
3. What happens during a day in your work life?
4. What advice would you give to someone [going through whatever stage you're in now: starting your career/ becoming a new manager/transitioning industries]?
5. What makes a résumé stand out to you?
6. When you feel overwhelmed at work, what do you do to stay resilient?
7. What do you believe contributed to your ability to progress in your career?
8. What is something you'd like to learn (or learn more about)?
9. What books or articles do you recommend I read?
10. What do you do for fun outside of work?

Maintain Contact

Though you may meet with a person only one time, you can continue the relationship by maintaining contact, even if it's something as small as sending an article you thought she might like. When someone I previously met with for an informational interview sends an update on her new job or life happenings, it brings me joy. I invested in that person with my time—one of my most valuable resources—and want to celebrate her success. Also consider sending congratulatory notes to your connections to celebrate *their* growth and successes.

You can use the following template to follow up on networking conversations or with an industry contact:

Dear X,

It was great to connect with you at X. I enjoyed our conversation and learning more about your career and role at [*company*]. I would welcome catching up again for a virtual coffee to hear what you're working on right now/ how I can best support you. What does your schedule like for the weeks of [*date*] or [*date*] (suggest times generally at least two weeks out)? I look forward to speaking with you again in the near future.

Most sincerely,

You

Closing the Network Gap

Here's something else to keep in mind: networks play a vital role in your career—but not everyone has equitable access to the kind of network that can do this. Your ability to be successful is based in part on where you grew up, where you went to school, and where you work. This is what LinkedIn termed the *network gap*, and they called attention to this because they learned from their platform how valuable an effective network can be.[1]

If you're someone who has not had access because of these factors, I hope this book will help you build the network you deserve.

If you've experienced benefits based on these factors, it's your responsibility and opportunity to support others. No matter where you are in your career, you can be a meaningful mentor. What an amazing thing you can do to serve others and create access—while navigating your own career growth.

CULTIVATING ADVISORS AND ADVOCATES

Where you stand in your career right now, you've likely worked hard, received recognition for significant projects you've completed, and have some thoughts on what you would like to do next, but you're not sure how to get there. This is where mentorship and sponsorship come in. And knowing the difference between the two is important: a mentor advises you, and a sponsor advocates for you. To advance your career, you'll need both.

Mentorship

It's possible you already have a mentor—in fact, you may have several. To level up how to benefit from your mentors' collective insights, create a board of advisors. These are the people you turn to for the best leadership and career advice.

A company has a board of advisors guiding them, giving them feedback, and helping them reach their full potential—and this is how they become even more successful. Think of yourself like an organization poised for transformational growth. This is how you'll thrive, too.

So, who belongs at the table with you? A well-rounded board of advisors includes different perspectives, industries, and roles—all with the goal of creating the strongest possible outcomes for the organization.

Unlike a company's board, there won't be formal meetings (hooray!) or performance report outs. People may not even know they're on your board of advisors.

Here's how to develop your board:

Step 1: Identify Your Advisors

First, make a list of everyone in your sphere of influence you consider to be someone you rely on for career and leadership guidance, or people you would like to turn to. Write down what industry they're in, their authority level, their expertise/focus/what they're known for, what you admire about them, and their relationship to you.

Now review the list for:

Which industry areas are missing (or overrepresented)? Think through new perspectives you can learn from, such as someone who has a similar role to the one you want next, but in a completely different industry or part of the world. It will be helpful to have an external or more objective perspective to your growth.

What is the influence factor of the people on your list? You want a mix of people you aspire to learn from, like the VP who took you for coffee and shared about their career, as well as people you can relate to, such as a peer. Be sure that each person leads from where they are and carries influence in the space they're in.

What is their expertise area? Consider how a person's focus area complements your own now—and what you'd like to be known for in the future. Having people with different areas of expertise can help you look at things holistically.

How have they supported you in the past? Note how they've championed you already and how you feel when you're seeking their perspective. If you feel energized, joyful, or motivated after you meet with them, that's a good start. Focus on practical aspects of the relationship, too, and how they support you with their time and network, such as whether they're a mentor or sponsor, or have met with you for an informational interview.

You don't have to personally know everyone on your board of advisors. If there is someone you admire and want to emulate, consider having them as a "member at large." It can be enough to think about what that person would do or what counsel they might offer you to help motivate you to be your best self.

Step 2: Cultivate Your Advisors

Plan for how you'll stay in contact with your list and nurture these relationships. I recommend adding a note to your calendar, quarterly or annually, so this remains a priority for you. The goal is to share updates about yourself and ask about them, too. You can draft an update about what you've been up to since you last connected and what you're proud of. You can include what you've accomplished or been working toward, and what you're looking to do or learn next.

It's important to show your advisors you care about their success, too. Send them a note when they've been recognized at their company or in the news. Ask them about their projects, their family, and their big dreams.

When you face a difficult decision or a crossroads, you need a door opened, or you're looking for feedback on an idea, they should be the people you reach out to first. If you've been keeping them apprised of your work and well-being, as well as asking about theirs, they'll be happy to take the call.

Step 3: Evolve Your Board as You Grow

For a traditional company board, there are term limits that ensure they get new ideas and perspectives as the organization's vision and needs change. You'll want this for yourself as you evolve and grow your career, too.

You'll need to spend time every few years reviewing your list and making sure it accurately reflects who you want to become. It's why you'll need to continue building your network and develop relationships with people you'd like to see on this list eventually.

Keep in mind that a board won't always agree with the choices you make. Consider their perspectives as a reflection of what they brought to the table and what you value about them—but remember it's your table.

You are your own best advocate for your career and growth, and you'll thrive with the right people supporting and challenging you in fulfilling your potential.

Sponsorship

Now that you have a board of advisors, you'll also need active investors in your career: sponsors. I've benefited from many sponsors who spoke on my behalf when I wasn't in the room. I can think of one sponsor in particular, Leslie, who was a high-level executive who invited me to work on a project with colleagues far more senior than me. She believed I would get things done and sought me out for other cross-functional teams, too. When I later was being considered for a promotion, I asked if she would put in a good word for me. She agreed and I got the promotion.

Sounds great, right? It is. Having other people on your side to advocate for you when you aren't in the room where decisions are made has the potential to change your career. So, let's dive into how to work with a sponsor.

How to Identify a Sponsor

Before anything else, you must understand that sponsors are in the rooms where decisions happen. They have power to make decisions, they know about your work, and they are willing to spend their political capital on you. They are the bosses you've heard about who invest deeply in people's careers and have their staff members' backs in times of challenge.

Take a few minutes to write down a list of people at your company who could be potential sponsors for you.

How to Cultivate a Sponsor

After you have identified potential sponsors, it's important to realize that it takes time to develop meaningful connections with them. Carla Harris, vice chairman at Morgan Stanley and a speaker on career development, explains the concepts of performance currency and relationship currency in her TED Talk, "How to Find the Person Who Can Help You Get Ahead at Work."[2] Every time you perform above expectations, you earn performance currency. This is how you build your reputation and get noticed. It may even attract someone who could be your sponsor, but that is not guaranteed on its own. Relationship currency, on the other hand, reflects the investment you make in building connections with people you work with, and this is why it's valuable. You want people to know you—and your work—so that when you approach them, it is easy for them to say yes.

What to Ask a Sponsor

You don't always have to formally ask someone to sponsor you. Ideally, they're already inspired by your work and speak up on your behalf without you even knowing. The key here is that you must have already done the great work to have something to stand on. If you're asking someone to formally take on this role, it is important to be clear about what your goals are and what your ask is. A sponsor, unlike a mentor, usually isn't the one helping you figure out what your next step is, as much as helping open the door for you.

Things to Know About Sponsors

When you advocate for someone else, they become an extension of you. It's important to find sponsors who believe in your potential. Sponsors, like mentors, don't have to be just like you, though. After all, the goal should be to make the table more expansive and inclusive.

I often try to use my influence to support other people's careers. I don't do it for everyone, though. Yes, performance and relationship currencies play a major part, and it's also about timing. If you approach someone to be a sponsor and they don't feel it's the right time or they're the right fit, don't get dejected. You'll have to put yourself out there and follow through (a lot!) for your good work to be noticed by a sponsor who will be willing to do the same for you.

CONSIDERING WHAT'S MOST IMPORTANT IN A NEW ROLE

As you determine next steps in your career, you'll have choices to make on how a potential role aligns with your goals. This doesn't mean you have to find the "perfect" job—it's determining the right career move that gets you closer to what's most important to you. In order to grow professionally, you may find you need to leave your company, or you may decide to choose a new industry. I know this from my personal experiences.

When I got to the point in my mid-career when I felt like my role was no longer a fit for me, I interviewed at various institutions to see what else would be possible for me. On several occasions, I was offered the job, and I turned them all down. In every instance, I attributed it to something bizarre about the manager, location of the institution, significant relocation for our family, lack of opportunities for my husband, or the like.

Though all of these are valid reasons, I knew in my heart that I was running away from something. Running *away* often comes from a place a fear. Running *toward* something comes from a place of strength. So I decided to wait until I was clear on what I was running toward.

For additional perspective, I sought counsel from my former boss and mentor, Bob. I talked about jobs that were one level above in the org chart, and he listened and thoughtfully offered advice. During one of our conversations, he offhandedly said, "You know, I think you could be looking at associate vice president jobs, if you wanted to." I remember thinking in that moment how much his feedback meant to me. This was, after all, the role he had been in when I first met him—the job I wanted to have "someday"—and he thought I was ready.

I started to interview for roles at the highest organizational levels, managing complex teams and multimillion-dollar budgets, and, more important, believed I could do the job. Women can tend to downplay their skills and accomplishments. It wasn't about a title; it was the opportunity to lead an organization at the enterprise level with all the challenges and learning that came with it. My own thinking had been limiting me from doing exactly what I wanted to do. I got caught up in what I was "supposed to do," both in terms of my aspirations and my industry choices. And so, I ran toward something that got me closer to who I wanted to become.

Through each career transition I've made, I've learned that you can love something and still leave it in order to grow.

When you're deciding on a new job, here are four questions to consider before saying yes.

1. **How will your day-to-day life change?** With each new role
    you take, your daily routine will likely change in some
    way—even if you stay in the same organization. You may
    be expected to relocate or travel frequently. You might
    have a longer commute or no commute. You may manage
    a team for the first time or manage a larger team. If you're
    transitioning to a new industry, you may have additional
    skills or certification you need to work toward in the
    evenings or on weekends. Try to get a sense of how this job
    will change what your life looks and feels like in the short-
    and long-term.

2. **How will this role create new learning for you?** You want to
    be in a position where you can use your strengths—and
    develop new ones. A job should offer clear opportunities to
    learn, both formally and informally. Think through what
    skills you want to develop, what experiences you want to
    have, and who will be teaching you, and ensure that the
    new job can help you attain at least some of these goals.
    Ideally the organization shows interest in developing you,
    rather than you having to do this all on your own. Take
    note: even experts should pursue continuous learning.
    After all, learning influences your personal and financial
    well-being, as well as your happiness.[3]

3. **Who will your new boss be?** Who you work for and with is
    extremely important to your happiness and success in the
    role. (You might even be surprised I didn't list this question
    first!) When considering a new job, you want a boss who
    will positively challenge you—and have your back. Your
    boss is also ultimately responsible for your performance
    evaluations and compensation, which determine your
    success at the company and your financial well-being,

respectively. During the interview process, ask questions to get a sense of their values, how they approach their work, their expectations of team members, and what is most important to them.

4. **Who do you want to become?** This is the question I asked you at the start of the book! It shows up throughout the chapters because it's tied to your career and leadership—and to who you are as a person. Your Bold Moves should lead you to what you want your future to look like and who you're becoming. Will this job give you space to pursue what's most important to you in your life? When you think about your life in 5, 10, 15 years, what does it look like for you? Work should fit into your life, not the other way around.

Applying for a Job as a Woman

There is one thing I want to tell all women: you don't have to meet all the qualifications to apply for a job. Studies show women are less likely to apply for jobs for which they perceive themselves to be underqualified.[4] The experiences you already have and the strengths you would bring to a new role are often more than enough to apply. Thoughtfully consider how your skills align with the role you are interested in, but don't force yourself to consider only 100 percent matches. After all, a new job should bring opportunities to learn new things.

When you find a job you're interested in and you meet some of the expectations, but not all, don't decide for the employer if you should be hired. Put yourself out there as a candidate and tell the story in your cover letter of why you are the right person for this job. *It's their job to choose the best person for their organization—it's yours to give yourself the opportunity to be considered.*

EXPLORING ENTREPRENEURSHIP

When I was a child, I often had to fill out forms that said what my parents did. It was easy to describe my mom's work: she was a teacher. When I listed what my dad did, his answer was always more complicated. His primary role during my childhood was running a global dialysis business he built. When I asked what he did, his response was entrepreneur. I didn't even know what an entrepreneur was, little less how to spell it. I was embarrassed and told him that was a made-up thing. Eventually he acquiesced and would say he was a chemical engineer, which seemed like a real job I could understand. That became what I would say whenever asked.

Entrepreneurs are still told they have made-up careers, and their dreams are dismissed by others—even by the people who love them most. It's not always intentional. Some people want to protect loved ones from failure. Or maybe, like me, they're kids who want to have something "normal" to say about their parents on Career Day. That's the thing about entrepreneurship, though: you have to believe in yourself when no one else does.

Looking back now, it probably broke my dad's heart that his daughter didn't value what he said he was. But then I grew up and I had an "and" career, which I defined as having two distinct careers that were important to me—and one of them was being an entrepreneur. It was a big deal for me to write that at first. It took me several years to fully embrace that I was running a business and building a movement. I loved what I did in nonprofit executive leadership and fundraising, and I also loved supporting others in leveling up their careers and leadership. For me, being engaged in both of these aspects of my work and life enabled me to be stronger in each role.

People often ask me how I started building my business. It wasn't an intentional process for me at first, and I definitely needed external prodding. Many years ago, when LinkedIn blogging was starting to take off, I decided to write an article. I can still remember how nervous I was when I pressed "publish" for the first time. I couldn't sleep that night wondering how it would be received. To my delight, people started to comment and share. From there, I made a commitment to put myself out there again, but it took nearly six months. Over time, I got a bit bolder and pitched an external publication. My first big byline was in *Huffington Post*. Around that same time, Terri, one of the donors I worked with in my "day job," pulled me aside at an event and said, "It's time for you to create a website and get organized." I remember being both shocked and surprised. It was not something I had considered previously, but I admired her career and counsel, so I told her I'd reach back out to take her to breakfast and get more of her insights.

Following that breakfast meeting a few weeks later, I felt better prepared. I registered for a domain name and developed my own website. I had no experience in any of this, so thank goodness for friends with technology and marketing experience, and Squarespace tutorials. When I was ready to get more serious about writing, I hired a writing coach, and from there, a business I didn't originally know I wanted to create started to grow.

Even after running a business for several years, I still hesitated to call my work a business and even downplayed that this side hustle existed. Thanks to Christy, an encouraging friend, who said one night over dinner, "Shanna, this isn't a side hustle, this is a *side career*." I realized she was right. And I've called it that ever since.

As you can see, starting my business took a lot of encouragement from others. Launching a side hustle or full-time entrepreneurship career isn't for everyone but could be a great way to explore whether entrepreneurship full-time is right for you. It can also create multiple income streams (and to have one for backup) or expand on your strengths.

If you have an idea for a business but aren't sure what to do first or you're starting out now and figuring your way, here are four things to consider.

1. **Be clear on your why.** If you're starting a business in addition to your day job, it will require nights and weekends. Are you willing to put in that extra time? If so, figure out what motivates you. What do you hope to accomplish? What are you willing to sacrifice to achieve your goals? Think through these questions to establish your why.

2. **Decide what you need to start.** One of the misconceptions about starting a business is that you need to have it all figured out before you start. This isn't true. My business has evolved over time, and through experience I clarified how it serves others. You don't need a logo or website on day one, but you should create timelines to work toward so people know who you are, what you offer, and how to find you. I didn't formalize an LLC for my business for the first few years.

3. **Explore how your day job will support you (or not).** Unfortunately, you can't presume that everyone will be excited for you. In some more traditional organizations, they may see your side hustle as competition for your time and energy. It will be up to you to clarify to your employer that you are not mixing your time or resources—and in some cases, how your new endeavor can be complementary to your daytime work.

4. **Tell the world.** It may feel awkward to talk openly about yourself, but you're the best marketer for what you're doing. Sharing this proudly is a Bold Move. Plus, you're going to need others to support your growth. Consider sending out emails or posting videos on social media so you can get

people excited about your new venture. Be specific with how people can help you—whether that means hiring you directly, buying your products or services, or suggesting referrals.

If you decide you're excited to try entrepreneurship part-time or make the leap full-time, there's no such thing as the "perfect time." So go ahead and make your Bold Move and start now!

• • •

Here's something I didn't fully understand about careers when I started: your choices don't have to be permanent. You can change industries, even if you spent years gaining experience in a particular area. You can switch back and forth between working for a company and running your own company. When it comes to advancing your career, you don't have to have it all figured out—but you do have to start somewhere, so why not start today?

BOLD MOVES TO MAKE NOW

Identify three people you want to build relationships with and make plans to reach out to them.

Send to each of your mentors a note and career update so you can stay connected. If you don't have any yet, who could you engage further in your growth?

Make a list of the skills you want to learn or cultivate within yourself to advance your career.

The Power of Uplifting Others

I wanted to be a collegiate cheerleader. Their fancy outfits, powerful moves, ability to bring joy to others, and the drive to cheer others on was inspiring to me.

Every game, they would dress up and show up. I mean, really *show up* as they bravely flipped into the air. I spent most of my life thinking I hadn't done a single thing to make that dream come true (other than wearing one Halloween costume). But eventually, I realized I *am* a cheerleader, because you don't have to flip over backward to cheer others on.

There's real science behind cheering on and uplifting others. Research by Emma Seppälä of Stanford University and author of *The Happiness Track* shows how giving to others brings you joy.[1] She explains that sharing joy can come in the small moments of your day or the biggest relationships of your life. It starts with finding joy in the power of connection and embracing it.

How you connect with and uplift others may change over time as you enter different stages of your career and life, such as supporting women just starting their careers, working mothers, and grieving friends. What will not change is your ability to make a meaningful difference through your actions in caring for others, no matter what stage you're in. Let's explore different ways you can create uplifting connection for yourself and others in your life starting right now.

CREATE MOMENTS OF GENUINE CONNECTION

The very first step to creating moments of genuine connection is being present with others. Throughout any given day, you interact with many people. You have a choice in how you make those seemingly trivial encounters a bit more meaningful for yourself and others. It can be as simple as saying "hello" and "thank you" or engaging in a brief conversation. Research shows your happiness increases when you connect with others—and I think it might even have the power to do more than that.[2]

Back when I commuted daily, I often ran late for the train. (I run late for lots of things, if we're keeping it real.) One day I did my usual sprint to the train home and watched the train doors close just as I arrived. The next train was nearly 30 minutes later, so I sat down on the nearby bench to wait. A well-dressed woman also sat down on the bench and complimented me on my dress. I could easily have let it be just a nice compliment and continued with my day, but something inspired me to keep talking with her. After all, I had a while to go until my next train. I asked her what industry she worked in and learned she was chief marketing officer at a global firm. We ended up talking about our work, families, and life. Before I knew it, the next train pulled into the station, and we exchanged cards before parting ways. I could have ended the connection at that point, but instead I wrote her an email that evening to say it would be fun to continue the conversation over coffee. She responded with an invitation to her club for breakfast, and we shared a meaningful dialogue about career choices, navigating office politics, working motherhood, and maintaining friendships as adults. For months afterward, I ran into her occasionally on the train or in neighborhood coffee shops, and we always exchanged pleasantries.

Over a year later, we bumped into each other again, this time while I was on one of my first masked outings after being allowed in stores again during the Covid-19 pandemic. Despite the face coverings, we recognized each other from afar and said hello. I could have maintained a surface conversation, as you do when you run into people in passing, but I talked to her about the podcast I had started during the pandemic and watched as she added it to her Apple Podcast library. We picked up our correspondence again via email, met occasionally for coffee, and Lisa was one of the first people I told when I got the book deal.

This story included lots of Bold Moves for me. Maybe your Bold Move is saying hello to a person you pass on the street or authentically complimenting someone on her dress. If this is new for you, that's a big deal. If that's something you already do, try asking a question more than the usual "How are you?" You can ask someone what they're reading, which is usually aligned with what a person enjoys or values, to tap into something deeper with them. (You might end up with a great book recommendation, too!) My favorite question to ask is, "What has been the highlight of your week?" It leads to both sharing joy and finding meaning. Though it embarrasses my husband to no end, I even do this in the grocery checkout line when the cashier seems to want to engage in a conversation.

Making a proactive connection with others involves choosing to be intentional with your attention. Think about all the times you've had a conversation with the person at the table next to yours at the coffee shop. Or were you the person with your earbuds in? People tend to both underestimate how much they'll enjoy connecting with a stranger and worry too much about how the other person will respond.[3] The reality is the worst thing that might happen is the other person says no, ignores you, or looks surprised.

In fact, in one research study, participants were asked to interact with strangers once a day over five days, and in the end, 99 percent of participants found at least one conversation "pleasantly surprising"—and 40 percent of them communicated with one of the strangers again. Going forward, I hope you'll consider the gift of a seemingly random connection with other people. And, just in case you need even more motivation to try this, research shows even minimal interactions with strangers leads to a happiness boost![4]

You can get started with this today. In the bottom of your work bag, you can likely find a business card for a person you keep meaning to reach out to. Call this person or send an email to reconnect. Go ahead and initiate a conversation with the person you see watering their flowers while you're out walking your dog. Ask the barista what his name is—and remember it.

You leave impressions every day on everyone around you, and when you share kindness with others it becomes a part of you and a part of them. Kindness creates a connection between people, and I think we can all agree that we can use more kindness in our lives.

SUPPORT OTHER WOMEN

Though I encourage joyfully connecting with everyone, there is a special power that comes from women supporting other women.

As a Xennial (microgeneration between Generation X and millennials), I grew up in a time when women didn't always help other women.[5] Or looked at in a different light, they supported other women in the best way they knew with the information they had at the time. Some women were afraid to help other women because there was a perceived (or real) scarcity of roles available. Others felt that women should not get extra support, because they hadn't received any during their own careers. I always found this way of thinking troublesome. If I disrespected or undermined others because that had happened to me, I would not be the kind of leader, colleague, or friend I aspire to.

Instead, I want to be a part of changing the narrative—by opening every door I can for other women, even if those doors had been closed to me. And I'm happy to say that many others appear to be moving in this direction too.

Bring Other Women up with You

It is my responsibility to bring other women up with me and to work toward successful outcomes for *all* women.

Here's what this looks like in everyday life:

Amplify other women's voices in meetings when they get shut down. Point out when women's ideas are missed or "borrowed" and redirect the conversation back to what they shared.

Give credit to women for their projects. Help other women shine by pointing out what their projects did to help your team or the organization.

Share salary information to help promote transparency and reduce the gender wage gap. To reach gender pay equity, women need to know what to ask for in the context of their industry and role.

Ask for an extra event ticket to bring someone you mentor or want to open doors for. Once you have made it to the place where you can open doors for others, help them get into the rooms that can advance their careers.

Talk with other women about your experiences. When you vulnerably share about what you've faced in your career, you can give other women insights they can learn from—and help them feel less alone.

If you're looking for ways to connect with other women, consider joining a professional women's network. I've been fortunate to benefit from many groups that have helped elevate my career and create opportunities for others, including Luminary, HeyMama, and Ellevate Network. In addition to the psychological benefits of having positive relationships with other women, it can also help you achieve your goals.

Beyond bringing other women up with you, this is about *building* other women up around you. When another woman chooses to make her Bold Move, celebrate her. We rise together.

Champion Working Moms

As a new working mother, I often felt I had to hide what I was doing to make it all happen at work and at home. I didn't talk openly about negotiating with my husband about who would leave work early for the unexpected snow day closing. I didn't share that I rearranged my business travel schedule to take the overnight flights to Europe so I could be home for one more family dinner. I spoke in hushed tones when school called (of course, calling me as the mother, even though my husband was also listed as a contact) about something that had happened that day. I meticulously dressed and did my hair and makeup each day so I would look like I had it all together—

even on the days when I'd done enough parenting and household responsibilities that I had practically worked a full day before arriving at the office. Some of this was my perception about how women succeeded at having it all—and some of it was real gender bias. Joan C. Williams of University of California Hastings College of the Law and author of *What Works for Women at Work* (one of my favorite books!) created the term "maternal wall" to describe a type of bias when people view mothers or pregnant women as less competent and less committed to their jobs.

You don't have to be a mother yourself, or want to have children, to champion working mothers. Whether a woman has just returned to work after parental leave or has been navigating working motherhood for years, she will benefit from your support.

Speak Up for Moms

Part of the bias of the maternal wall is that mothers aren't perceived to be as dedicated to their careers. Correcting this means addressing what's being said and what's not being said. Shut down any comments about working moms who rush out of the office at 5 p.m. Truth talk: I once was that person who whispered about working moms leaving early and how they can't possibly be doing their jobs. That memory reminds me of why it's so important now for me to share with others how to support working mothers. Though you may not directly experience what others do as a working parent, show compassion—and advocate for them. It shouldn't fall only to working mothers to speak up about office policies that negatively affect them. This isn't about special privileges: workplace culture should prioritize everyone's well-being.

Be Mindful of Scheduling

I've been known to swoop into conference rooms like James Bond ducking under a closing steel door as I tried to navigate school drop-off, commuting to work, and getting to that early morning meeting. In some workplaces, there are parameters on when meetings can be scheduled to be mindful of the demands on people's time. Let's be real, no one really likes rushing in for an early morning meeting, so this is more inclusive for everyone! Just as mornings can be a balancing act, so can the rest of the workday. Meeting times often need to be changed to keep up with unexpected demands of the workday, and though these changes can cause friction for everyone, they can be an added challenge for caregivers. Mothers may have set aside time to pump or need to leave early to get to parent-teacher conferences. If you're changing a scheduled meeting, consider how it might affect everyone and give as much advance notice as possible.

If you're not sure how to support a working mother, ask her! She will be grateful for the acknowledgment, even if she doesn't yet have the answer figured out.

SUPPORT OTHERS IN TIMES OF NEED

As important as it is to share connection in moments of joy, there is also power in sharing connection in difficult situations. In moments of tragedy, illness, or death, you cannot take away pain and suffering, but you do have the ability to make things just a bit lighter or more comfortable.

You may feel unsure of how to help a grieving friend or worry you're going to do or say the wrong thing. Preparing for these moments with grace is a Bold Move. Here are ways you can support a friend or colleague who is going through a difficult time.

There's no perfect moment. It's natural to feel nervous about reaching out. Don't wait. If we've learned anything about life, it's that there is never a perfect moment, and no moment is

promised to us. Your friend or colleague needs you now—
even your imperfect self. Show up for them.

Offer, don't ask. So many times, well-intentioned people say,
"Let me know if there's anything I can do." Or "How can
I help?" But in the moment, it's much more helpful to tell
someone what you'll do to be helpful. For example, say, "I'd
like to bring you dinner every Wednesday night, or Tuesday
if you prefer. This way you'll have something you can count
on. Does that work for you?" Something like this is a gift in so
many ways, including saving the person the energy of having
to think about these decisions.

Let them feel heard. Your goal is not to make them feel better.
Instead, your job is to let them feel heard. You can't erase what
they've been through, nor should you try. If they want to talk,
listen. If they feel like being silent, honor this. Whatever they
need in that moment, hear them.

Don't compare experiences. We're taught that empathy means
relating to what someone is feeling, but compassion is
more important in grief. Even if you, too, have experienced
something tragic and difficult, it's best not to presume that
it's the same as what this person is feeling. Sharing your own
story without being invited to could feel like comparison, or
worse, competition. All experiences of loss are difficult. Focus
only on what your friend is going through right now. That
said, your friend may identify differently with people who
have experienced something similar.

Be mindful of your own perspectives on grief and death. It's
safer to keep the comments to yourself about how everything
happens for a reason or a person who is dying will be "better
off." There are many different beliefs about death and dying,

and you wouldn't want to unintentionally upset the grieving person by professing your beliefs. If they're interested in your perspective, they may ask, but don't offer.

Use language carefully. Pay attention to the cues from the person you're talking to and try to emulate their language or tone in how they're talking about their experience. Follow their lead and do the same so you can be what they need at that time. I also try to say the name of the person who is ill or has died. It feels like a small way to honor them and allow comfort for the person who is grieving to speak about them too, if they want to.

Grief and death make us uncomfortable, which is understandable. There's so much uncertainty in these moments. It is this very vulnerability, of not always knowing the right thing to say or do, that connects us to others and is the reason we show up anyway.

CONNECT PEOPLE IN YOUR NETWORK

Whether in the happiest times or most difficult moments, our connection to others is powerful. Once you take the time to build meaningful relationships with others, you'll be able to multiply this goodness by connecting people in your network with each other, too.

I've always loved connecting people. Many of my introductions have led to mentorship, jobs, and even marriages! I have a special place in my heart for connecting people I think would enjoy each other as friends. When you connect two people, you're saying, I believe in you and want good things for both of you. I've connected two friends who live in the same neighborhood and work in similar industries. I've connected two friends who share educational backgrounds and personal values. I've connected a friend with someone who has the job she wants to be in someday. And I've made it

76

a point to introduce team members to people in my network for coaching or job opportunities. As you grow in your career, it's especially important to help others who may be just starting their own.

If you've been more of a reactive connector (when someone needs something specific), you can shift to being more proactive by offering to make introductions when there seem to be natural points of overlap. It's a way to add value to people in your network, and I like to think it makes the world a better place.

Now that you're ready to build connections within your network, it's important to make these connections the right way, which includes the following:

Ask Permission to Connect

Earlier in my career, I would get so excited to introduce two people I knew would enjoy each other that I would write a thoughtfully personalized email introduction for two people and proudly send it out, waiting for the magic to happen—except sometimes it didn't. I might unintentionally surprise someone with my request, or there might be nuances I wasn't aware of related to the request. I learned the hard way that the most important rule of connecting two people is simple: ask first. Asking permission gives people the option to accept or decline without making things awkward.

Let's say you're talking with a friend or colleague who's looking for an important connection to advance her career or business, and there's someone in your network who could be an influential contact for her. Go ahead and reach out to the more senior person or the one of whom you'll be asking a favor. Write to only that person and ask if they would be willing to meet with, connect with, or whatever it is that you're hoping for with your friend. Include a two-or-three-sentence bio about the person, how you know them, and why you think they should be connected. You can further personalize this based on your relationship. The most important part: give the recipient an out clause. This might sound like, "If this isn't the right connection for you or the right time, I certainly respect how much you have going on." Including a sentence like this gives the person on the receiving end the opportunity to decline without having to explain themselves, and this approach preserves your relationship with them.

Host the Connection

After you get permission, send an email introduction. You're the host of this connection, much like at a dinner party, so share something about each person to give the other a sense of who they're being connected to and why you're connecting them. You may include what makes them special, the things you admire about them, or how you first became acquainted. I take great pride in connecting people within my network, so I want my initial request to reflect that joy.

At the close of the email, I like to say, "I'll leave it to you two to connect directly from here," making it clear that the next steps are up to them.

Here's a template you can use for this:

Dear [*Name*]:

It's my pleasure to introduce two terrific people, and I've copied you both on this email.

[*Two-or-three-sentence intro of Person 1—can include title/how you know them/what you admire about them/ mutual area of interest*].

[*Two-or-three-sentence intro of Person 2—can include title/how you know them/what you admire about them/ mutual area of interest*].

I thought to introduce both of you because [*reason you're connecting them/what the ask is*], and I know [*Person 2*] can learn a lot from you, [*Person 1*].

I'll leave it to you two to connect directly from here.

Best to you both.

[*Your Name*]

Follow Through on the Connection

You can differentiate yourself in the connection process by how you follow through.

Here's something many people miss: establishing who follows up first after the email introduction has been sent and when. If the connection is to ask for a favor for you or you're the more junior of the two people, you should reach out first—and promptly. It shows respect to the other person's time you're requesting and diligence to the host's effort.

Following the connection, graciously acknowledge the connector and move them to the BCC line. This lets them know you've followed up and saves their inbox. It's also always well received when you take time to send a note to this connector to let them know how much you enjoyed the conversation. You can let them know of any next steps or something you've learned. They'll remember this the next time you ask for a connection.

When following these steps, you'll be seen as someone who understands the power of positive connections.

• • •

You have the gift of bringing joy to the world, just by being yourself. Even to one person. Go share your gifts.

BOLD MOVES TO MAKE NOW

Reach out to someone you've been meaning to reconnect with.

Look for an opportunity in your daily life to embrace curiosity to create a genuine moment of connection with others.

Send a note (bonus if handwritten!) or text to another woman to cheer her on.

Invest in Yourself

The most important investment you can make is in yourself. When I say "invest," I mean giving your time, attention, or energy to something with the expectation of a worthwhile result.

I suspect you are known as someone who gives your energy to making the world and workplace around you a better place. Consider this: *you* are worth your own investment, too—and this means you have to make time for the things that matter most.

By prioritizing and investing in your personal growth while advancing your career and developing as a leader, you demonstrate to yourself that you are worth the same time, attention, and energy that you give to others. Remember, you have to first invest in yourself, so others will invest in you, too.

In this chapter, we'll explore how to focus on the right things, create habits to sustain you, and value this investment in yourself—even when you're pulled in different directions.

FOCUS ON YOUR BEST AND HIGHEST USE OF TIME

To focus on the right things, you have to understand how to measure your best and highest use of time. For many years, I have had a small index card above my desk in my office to help me focus on my top priorities (see figure). On the card is a rectangle divided into four quadrants: "important/urgent," "not urgent/important," "urgent/not important," and "not urgent/not important." This visual reminds me that how we spend our time is a choice.

Focus on What's Important at Work

Urgent/ Important *best and highest use of time	Not Urgent/ Important *best and highest use of time
Urgent/ Not Important	Not Urgent/ Not Important

Prioritization Matrix

This quadrant visual is based on the Eisenhower Matrix, developed by former President Dwight Eisenhower and popularized by Stephen Covey.

Let's review the quadrants and how they can help you prioritize: "important" refers to a project's value, and "urgent" refers to a project's timing. With this in mind, "urgent/important" and "not urgent/important" will be your top priorities.

You can sense what is both urgent/important, and you're likely spending time on the things in this quadrant, which include time-sensitive issues, crises, deadline-driven work, external pressures on top priorities, and the last-minute rush for big projects.

The things that are not urgent yet important tend to slip lower on your to-do list, because there isn't a specific deadline or other issue require your attention sooner—but they're still important.

To make progress on these "not urgent/important" priorities, you need to plan for them. First, define or set a date that you will complete the project. Then estimate the amount of time it will take you to do the work, and add these blocks to your calendar.

Here are two examples of how to implement this strategy in your work:

Scenario #1: Developing a New Initiative for the Organization

Next month, you'll be presenting to a committee of your boss and peers on a new initiative for the organization that you've been working on. In the meantime, your inbox is full, and you have a stack of documents to review that are due by the end of the week. You still have plenty of time to develop this project, even though you know it will take a lot of time to finish drafting and preparing for the presentation.

STRUCTURE

1. Set aside an hour each week for the next four weeks to work on the presentation deck and rehearse your remarks.
2. Instead of writing on your calendar something abstract like the name of the initiative or "work on project," divide the work into four even parts and label your calendar accordingly.
3. With protected time on your calendar during the workday, you will avoid late-night prep sessions. When you sit down

to do the work, you can refer to the specific part of the project instead of scrambling to figure out which parts you've completed and which one to work on next.

Scenario #2: Working Toward a Promotion

To prepare to ask for a promotion, you want to rewrite your job description and prepare materials about your accomplishments to share with your boss, but there may not be a true timeline for presenting this to your boss.

STRUCTURE

1. Create a self-imposed deadline. Determine when you want to show the materials to your boss and work backward from there to prepare your materials.
2. Put the deadline on your calendar, along with two 30-minute blocks of time when you'll review and prepare.
3. When you have these blocks on your calendar, you will be better positioned to prioritize this work—and your growth—during the workday instead of trying to fit it in between your other meetings.

You can adapt this type of planning structure to focus on whatever your top priority scenario is amid other deadline-driven projects.

• • •

Here's one more tip to keep making progress on your priorities: make the time that you have work for you. Many time experts will tell you if something on your to-do list can get done in 15 minutes or less, do that thing first. While I'm no time expert, that's not how I approach things. If you have 15 minutes to get something done (it may be your only free 15 minutes that day between meetings), I suggest asking yourself this question: What is one thing you can do to move forward something that is important but not urgent? Sure, you won't complete it, but you can and will make progress.

Keep this in mind for other examples of things that are not urgent yet are important: building your network and other relationships, learning, and rest. This is the basis of this chapter: investing in yourself by understanding what is the best and highest use of your time and prioritizing these things accordingly.

While we would like to think we spend most of our time on the important things in our life, the reality is that we all actually spend much of our time with the urgent/not important tasks, or worse, the not urgent/not important. This includes emails, some meetings, everyone else's projects, scrolling through Instagram, and requests where someone else could have figured out the situation on their own. Sometimes these things are handed to us, and sometimes we do them to ourselves. When you're feeling most overwhelmed or anxious, refer to the diagram and realize you've likely allowed other people's urgency to become your own.

In this case, you need to determine which things you can *delegate*, *delay*, or *drop*.

Focusing on your best and highest use of time, the things that are urgent/important or are not urgent/important, allows you to preserve your energy. When these things don't get done, there are often consequences. When the "not urgent/not important" things don't get done, either you'll do them another time, or they just won't get done at all. When you keep pushing yourself to do all of them anyway, you're not able to show up as your best and highest self.

Here's what I want you to keep in mind as you sort through what you need to do when: This system isn't really about time. It's about who you are as a leader and what you value—which are both urgent and important.

DEVELOP BOLD MOVE PERFORMANCE PATTERNS

Your work responsibilities take up the majority of your day, but they don't have to be the majority of your life. Try to increase time for priorities that can help you grow as a person, which I call Bold Move Performance Patterns. These can include learning, hobbies, exercise, and rest. Developing new Bold Move Performance Patterns will enhance your happiness, health, and quality of life. And choosing to incorporate any of these into your life will provide you with an opportunity to focus on your own joy, reinforce to yourself that you are worth investing in, and build your creativity in the process.

Learn Something New

People who make a commitment to learn on their own will advance faster in their careers. There are many ways to do this, including attending conferences, lectures, or online training courses.

Another accessible (and less expensive way) to learn something new and invest in yourself is to read more. This is such an enjoyable way to learn but seems to be the first thing to go when we feel pressed for time. It feels luxurious, and sometimes frivolous, to sit down for an extended period of time "not doing anything." But research shows that reading reduces stress, in addition to building your knowledge.[1]

Choose books on topics that make you want to prioritize your reading time over other activities. If reading about art history brings you joy, then read that. It doesn't matter that it's not related to your career. If it will make you feel grounded and growing, then it's the right choice for you.

Reading doesn't have to be done solo, either, unless you prefer it that way. If book clubs are your thing, that's a great way to con-

nect with others and motivate yourself to read. You can also coordi-
nate with a reading buddy to discuss a book or topic. I have several
girlfriends I enjoy doing this with who live thousands of miles
away. It is a fun way to catch up and learn together at the same time.

If the idea of reading books still feels overwhelming, maybe
pick up a few articles on topics you enjoy. Give yourself 10 minutes
before work, during your commute, or before bed to get started.
Feeling like you can't even find 10 minutes to read? Try swapping
out scrolling through social media to read an article instead.

Podcasts are a solid alternative to reading. My podcast, *One
Bold Move a Day*, is a six-minute weekly podcast to help women
develop their careers and leadership that can be an easy place to get
started. To get the most benefits out of learning via audio, I encourage you to take notes. It changes your mindset from consuming
content to implementing ideas. If you're looking for a way to social-
ize what you're learning, form a podcast club to discuss episodes of
the group's favorite podcasts.

Find a Creative Outlet or Hobby

Another way to invest in yourself is to think about what kind of
projects you gravitate toward. How do you enjoy spending your
time when you're on vacation or not at work? These answers will
give you a better idea of the hobbies or creative outlets that will help
you thrive. Making time for these is important, even when you feel
stretched, because they will ultimately bring you more energy.

Your creative outlet could be baking, or pottery, or dancing, or
any one of a million ways to use your imagination. To incentivize
your behavior, try combining your creative time with something
else on your schedule that has a deadline. For example, maybe you
volunteer to make baked goods for the next neighborhood gath-
ering. Or maybe you take a friend or your child to the pottery stu-

dio with you. Maybe you color while you wait at your next doctor appointment. Research shows that creativity benefits your mental and physical health, including decreasing your stress levels and strengthening problem-solving skills.[2] While more time would be better, even five minutes is enough to achieve these benefits, so go ahead and get started somewhere.

Move Your Body

Are you the type of person whose exercise routine is deeply ingrained in your daily life, or do you go out of your way to avoid the gym in your building? I've fluctuated between periods of looking forward to exercising and wishing to do just about anything else. I'm the person who made fun of runners (because why would anyone do that on purpose?)—and then became a runner. I'm also the person who shunned the idea of group fitness (because it feels like everyone's watching you when you exercise in a group)—and then showed up four days a week at a studio. Maybe I'm not the best person to give advice on exercise, but the point is this: embrace where you are in the moment and work toward some kind of consistent movement because the benefits are incredible.

In fact, researchers at the University of Michigan found that more physical movement was generally connected with happiness, and that even as little as 10 minutes a day for one to two days a week could show results.[3]

So if you're someone who struggles to get started on those harder days, just remember that 10 minutes is enough. And, hey, you might be like me and realize halfway through the workout that you feel great and want to keep going.

And if you're struggling to get back out there, try this. When you get home from a run or finish a class you tried to get out of or weren't motivated to do, write yourself a note. It doesn't have to be long. Just say how you feel and maybe what you're proud of. Then the next time you feel like you don't want to get out there, look back at this note for the motivation you need to get it done.

Rest (and Take Your Vacation!)

Rest is often overlooked as a performance tool. The truth is that rest is essential to your ability to reach your full potential.

I have a habit my family and I refer to as "one more thing." You might have this, too. It's best described as a feeling that you can get just one more thing done before you finish up. And it can happen often. "Oh look, there's two minutes before the next meeting, I can get through just one more item on my to-do list." Or at the end of the workday, you have just one more email to send before you can shut off for the day. On the weekend, you can run just one more errand. No matter the example, you (and I) aren't really being efficient with time, we're often just trying to do more in less time. Doing this can come with negative consequences like being late to the next meeting, not giving the people in your life your full attention, or feeling exhausted all the time. All this hustling can lead to burnout and exhaustion—and it doesn't always get you where you want to go faster. At some point, you need to rest instead.

Rest comes in different formats and has many physical and mental health benefits, including an increase in your creativity,[4] decision-making,[5] and motivation,[6] while also decreasing your stress levels.[7] Let's look at a few different types of rest you can and should prioritize in your life.

Sleep

Before I get started, I want you to know that I'm not going to try to convince you to wake up at 5 a.m. to reach your big dreams or to have a specific morning routine. Instead, you can make Bold

Moves by simply creating a schedule that maximizes your ability to show up as your best self. To do this well starts with being mindful about the amount of sleep you get each night. I've been known to fall asleep on the floor . . . in the middle of the day. To be clear, this is not the kind of sleep I'm talking about. Your body will shut down when you're exhausted, but if you get to that point, you've likely missed several warning signs.

You are aware of the research on the importance of getting seven to eight hours of sleep a night,[8] and still this may not be enough of a motivator to do so because of everything you need to get done. Here's the thing: your lack of sleep affects more than just you—it also affects everyone around you, especially if you're a leader.[9]

Be proactive about your rest, so you can keep going and help others keep going, too.

Vacation

Many years ago, our family took a weeklong trip to the mountains. At the time, I worked for an organization where immediate communication was valued. I prided myself on being the most responsive colleague, but this took a toll on other aspects of my life. While we sat in the hotel room before our hike that first day, I looked at my phone and watched the number of messages in my inbox steadily rise. I knew myself well enough to know that I wouldn't be able to ignore this number as the day went on. While it might start as checking just one email, it could quickly turn into responding to multiple things. And even if I wasn't responding, every time I looked at my phone, it would divide my attention. So, I decided to turn off notifications from my work email. It would be as if it wasn't there at all.

As I switched the button to "off," I felt myself making a radical shift in how I spent my time with my family—both on that vacation and at home, because I still haven't turned those notifications back on.

The joys of vacation go beyond your time off, too. Research shows that anticipating your vacation boosts your happiness.[10] So before you go, spend time thinking about your trip. Visualize what you're most looking forward to. After you return, reminisce about your experiences by looking back at your photos or mementos you picked up that help you relive the positive moments.[11] (Research shows sharing your vacation memories has the potential to create positive feelings for others, too!)[12]

Vacation doesn't have to mean far-off locations and extravagant travels. It could be anything from spending your time hiking a trail to reading a good book, starting a new hobby, or trying out a recipe. You make choices about how to spend your time, wherever you are.

Maybe you've told yourself, "If I keep working hard and don't take time off, I'll be rewarded at work." After all, they'll see how dedicated you are, and you'll also score valuable face time with higher-ups. But here's the reality: People don't get promoted for dedication. They get promoted because they put in the work and make the case for themselves. Your well-earned time away from the office may be exactly what you need to put yourself into the frame of mind to excel in your job when you return and advocate for your growth in ways beyond answering emails. In case you need a little more convincing, studies have shown that people who take vacations are more likely to be promoted, so take your vacation![13]

Productive Rest

Sometimes the best solution in a specific situation is not to step away from everything, but to create more intention around what you're choosing to do, which is what I call "productive rest." To generate the best outcomes from productive rest, I suggest you set some guidelines about how you define rest, how long you plan to rest, and how you'll know when to keep going.

1. **Clearly define what "rest" means to you.** Decide which activities you're reducing or eliminating—and if you plan to replace them with something else. For example, if you decide you don't want to exercise, does this mean you're going to sleep in, or will you use the time to write in your journal or read instead?

2. **Determine what your timeline is.** Are you resting for an hour, a day, or a week? Be specific about the plan, so you work toward your own expectations. When you proactively set the timeline, you retain control over the process, instead of letting your exhaustion or frustration drive it.

3. **Be accountable.** When you're ready to get back to your work, invite others to help you stay accountable to your goals. Tell a friend or colleague about your plans so they can support you.

Then keep going. Step by step.

YOUR RETURN ON INVESTMENT (ROI) IN YOURSELF

The term "return on investment" (ROI) is thrown around a lot in the corporate world, and this concept applies to you, too. There's an ROI from your intentional investment in yourself that will benefit you today and in the future.

When you allocate time for learning, you will develop new skills that can enhance you personally and professionally. When you allocate time for creativity, you will renew your energy. When you allocate time for your health and well-being, you will build your physical and mental strength. All of these investments will support you in showing up as your best self.

Though this chapter is about investing in yourself in a metaphorical sense, there is a literal ROI that we should talk about, too. You should invest in yourself by asking for what you want and deserve financially and setting yourself up for financial success. Somewhere along the way when women were told to be nice, this also translated into our negotiations. Money became something that we weren't supposed to talk about. Our attitudes about money start when we are children, and those experiences can inform how we behave as adults.

Money can control you, or you can control it. If you live on your own, spend some time writing in a journal about what money means to you and what you hope to accomplish in the future. If you have a spouse or partner, talk openly with them about what money meant for you growing up, even if you never worried about having enough, and how you think about it now. Be clear about what you want to prioritize, the things you want to save for, and what your financial fears are.

Set yourself up for financial success by negotiating your salary, saving for retirement, and establishing financial goals. Get comfortable talking about money and asking questions about wealth. Learn how to give money to organizations that are important to you and find joy through philanthropy.

These investments in your skills, learning, health, and finances will help you create the life you want.

STOP FEELING GUILTY

The final step of investing in yourself is accepting where you are in the moment and letting go of guilt. Feeling guilty holds so many women back. It's something that comes up often in hushed conversations—if at all. In fact, it might be holding you back right now:

- You may feel guilty about working or guilty about parenting—or guilty for doing both.
- You may feel guilty for wanting to leave your employer.
- You may feel guilty about your ambition.
- You may feel guilty about taking time to do anything for yourself.
- You may feel guilty about putting your well-being first.
- You may feel guilty about resting.
- You may feel guilty about asking for too much.

Dear one, please stop doing this to yourself.

If you feel exhausted from doing it all, I'm with you.

But we all need to realize that this guilt limits us from taking on what is best for us and being our best selves.

Guilt steals your ability to be in the moment: it makes you think you should be somewhere else, doing something else, or worrying about the past. It robs you of your present and future joy.

You deserve great things. *Right now.*

Honor your decisions and free yourself from overthinking them.

You offer compassion and grace to everyone around you, and now it's time for you to offer it to yourself.

Let go of feeling guilty. In this moment. This is precious time we have here, and you deserve to live it fully.

BOLD MOVES TO MAKE NOW

Look back at the Prioritization Matrix to determine which activities this week belong in the Urgent/Important and Urgent/Not Important quadrants.

Choose at least one Bold Move Performance Pattern you will develop to invest in yourself.

Let go of one thing you are feeling guilty about.

Lead from Where You Are

People often ask me how they can advance their career and become a leader. Here's what I tell them: You are a leader. Yes, you.

Whether you manage people or not, you can be a leader. Leadership isn't about title or authority. It's the energy and purpose by which you lead yourself each day and how you serve others. That's what I mean when I say, "Lead from where you are." It starts with understanding everyone can lead regardless of their role in the organization. Approaching leadership this way means you have an opportunity to influence and inspire others no matter what stage of your career you're in. In time, you'll be ready to raise your hand for projects, and this can turn into more formal responsibilities at work.

It took time to figure out in my early career that you can lead without a fancy job title or being at the top of the org chart. I treated my first big job like I was still in school, where you're told what to do and evaluated (and rewarded) by how well you follow directions. After all, this was how women were taught the world works. I waited for a boss to tell me what to do or copied what colleagues did. Working this way got the job done, but it led to me feeling unaligned with my own actions. I kept meeting others' expectations, but I didn't feel like I was meeting my own. I didn't feel like myself.

Finding your authentic leadership style and voice will take time and practice, but the first step is to remember three things: you have the power to positively affect others, you have the ability to move projects forward, and sharing your voice matters—none of which requires a top leadership position.

Whether you're just entering the workforce or trying to navigate a large, complex organization 15 years into your career, it can be easy to confuse positional power—the formal authority a person holds—as the way to get things done in an organization. The truth is, titles (and corner offices) are great, but they will get you only so far. This is something I learned the very hard way in my first management role where I led the way I thought bosses should—by telling people what to do. Authority may get the job done, but you'll find yourself alone at the finish line.

When you build influence in your organization, collaborate with others, create value for your boss and your team, make your contributions known, and navigate workplace challenges, you're on the way to leading at any level. Let's dive into each together.

LEAD WITHOUT A TITLE

There are distinct ways you can develop your leadership approach even when you're only responsible for managing yourself. Leadership means serving others, so you'll want to build relationships to understand what your colleagues need, create opportunities to share your expertise, and be known as the go-to for advice and counsel.

Practice Active Listening

Though it seems fairly obvious that people want to be listened to, it can be hard to consistently give people your full attention in our always-on world. You can differentiate yourself by being someone who actively listens, which builds trust and relationships. Research shows that how you listen is even more effective in leading others than how you communicate.[1]

Active listening is more than helping someone else feel heard. It's being truly present and attentive. Do this by looking others in the eye (or at least the screen), and give them other nonverbal cues, such as minimizing your movement or other distractions. Repeat back to them what they've said, but not word for word. You can start by restating what they've said, "What I hear you saying is . . . ." This way, the person can clarify anything you've misunderstood or confirm that you heard them correctly. It shows you listened closely enough to be able to rephrase what they said to you, which required you to be fully present. Doing this can feel awkward at first, but don't worry—it doesn't sound as awkward to the person who's hearing it. In fact, it will feel exhilarating, because they will know you're truly listening to what they have to say. The benefits of listening go beyond making others feel valued—you'll also gain new information.

Understand the Organization

In addition to understanding your role, spend time learning what everyone else in the organization does, too. Try to find ways to connect the dots or collaborate across teams. I truly believe this is one of the ways I got to where I am in my career. Here's what this looked like for me: My boss told me to familiarize myself with the names of all the advisory board members for our organization.

After I reviewed all their names, I did a little homework on my own time about their backgrounds and companies. If I found news articles about the board members, I kept my boss informed. I also listened closely in internal meetings to the strategies my boss and my boss's boss were working on and found ways to add value. When I came across information of interest related to their strategies, I sent it along, and I did the same for my colleagues. As a bonus, my expanded knowledge helped me build connections in external meetings when people referenced their relationships with the board members.

Build Your Power

Don't give up your power by thinking you don't have any. When people seek you out in your day-to-day for advice or strategy because of what you know, this is a sign of what you bring to your organization. Being the colleague who is relied upon for her expertise gives you the ability to influence—regardless of where you may be in your organization. What you know and how you're willing to share it with others is your expert power. Consider how you can leverage your superpowers to contribute to your colleagues.

If you want to build your power further, continue developing your learning, too. Take a course online or attend webinars, read articles, listen to podcasts, and sit in on departmental meetings (even if they're not directly related to the work you do). You can develop this knowledge for good use for you and for your colleagues.

Collaborate with Others

Everyone wants to work in a collaborative work environment. Few organizations truly achieve it. Instead, people tend work in siloes, and as a result, breakdowns occur. It might sound idealistic, but the truth is *you* can make collaboration a reality in your workplace by leading the way for you and your colleagues.

Collaboration occurs when two or more people approach a situation or problem with their own ideas and then work together to develop an idea or solution that's even better than what one of them could have come up with on their own.

To build this kind of collaborative relationship with someone you work with, follow these three steps:

Step 1: Set up a meeting to discuss the problem you're trying to solve or develop the process you want to create. Practice actively listening to each other's ideas, not just representing your own. Sometimes collaboration means working so closely to develop a strategy that you eventually don't remember whose ideas were whose!

Step 2: Clearly define roles, frequency of communication, and how you'll relay updates with each other. I recommend creating a shared document for each project that outlines all of this information, so everyone involved can reference it later as needed.

Step 3: When there are roadblocks or issues, bring all parties back together to revise or create a new strategy, even if their part of the project is not directly affected. Having everyone invested in the solutions develops buy-in and provides additional perspectives.

Collaboration should be the goal for leaders, but many mistake this for cooperation and coordination. Cooperation is when two people work independently, but don't interfere or step on each other's toes. Coordination is when two people work toward a common goal, but not necessarily together. While it is possible to get things done without collaboration, you can create better work products together. And collaboration means everyone is invested in each other's success, versus solely their own, which contributes to a more positive work environment.

Support Your Colleagues

You spend much of your time at work, so it makes sense to find ways to support the people you spend this time with. Whether it's high-fiving a colleague when they secure a new client or sending someone a note when they're having a tough day, your colleagues will be grateful for your recognition and the opportunity for connection. Research shows that providing support for your colleagues affects your personal happiness, too.[2] (It apparently can also predict the likelihood of a promotion, though that shouldn't be your specific motivator!)

In one of my first jobs after college, I decided to start a tradition of bringing homemade treats to a staff meeting for every colleague's birthday. This coined me the nickname "Birthday Fairy," which I loved because I knew my gesture made the colleague feel special and brought everyone together. By choosing to support my colleagues in this small way, my actions created meaning. This was an early career lesson for me that the little things are the big things.

Don't wait until you're in a position of authority to help care for others. You may not be able to change your organization at a macro level, but you have the power to bring joy to others. Over time, you will be seen as the employee who can contribute by unifying the group toward a common cause. Here's the secret: as you progress on your leadership journey, your success is truly based on your team's success.

LEAD BY CREATING VALUE

There's a misconception that leadership means things happen *for* you or *to* you. In reality, leadership requires you to create opportunities. I'd like to share an example of this in action from early in my career.

After listening to colleagues' concerns about needing structure and role clarity for our growing external-facing team, I worked with my boss to create a process for the organization that had not existed before. This project leveraged my natural ability to understand how to align a donor's goals and expectations with what the organization needed to accomplish.

In reviewing names of new prospective donors and considering the fantastic colleagues I worked with (who all had different strengths), I paired donors and staff for a mutually beneficial and positive working relationship. I was basically solving a puzzle with tremendous upside for the organization—and I was good at it. This work both fulfilled my interest in developing solutions to raise more money and benefitted my colleagues, too. It's also real-life proof that you really don't have to manage people to positively influence them and their work outcomes. (And as a bonus, even 15+ years later, the work I did on this project remained part of my role in every subsequent organization I worked for.)

If you want to create opportunities to show your leadership abilities but you're not sure where to get started, consider which activities bring you the most energy or what problems you think you can solve for the organization. Remember those superpowers we talked about earlier and put them into practice! Some ways you can do this include sharing ideas with your boss about how you believe you can contribute to the team or showing your interest in taking on new challenges. If you don't have the opportunity to work on something specific right away, that's fine! Whatever tasks you're given, bring enthusiasm to the work that you do. Value isn't only made by the outcomes of your projects, but what you put into them.

That being said, when you raise your hand or suggest something you'd like to work on, know that not all ideas are created equal. Keep in mind the concept of "wise productivity." If you volunteer for a project that benefits you without understanding how it will affect your colleagues or ignore others' concerns, you've missed the mark. If you overdo your efforts to support the organization to your own detriment, you won't be successful either. The goal isn't to burn out while you build.

As you lead from where you are in the organization, you'll start to be recognized (in a good way!) for your ideas and work product— and it will become even more important for you to make sure your value is seen by leaders and decision makers in your organization.

MAKE YOUR CONTRIBUTIONS KNOWN

It's your responsibility to make sure your boss and other higher-ups know the value of your contributions. Even if you're a superstar in your role, you can't rely on this being front of mind for other people, including those who determine your future growth opportunities. This means you'll need to gracefully and consistently communicate your worth. And you can't afford to miss this part, because it plays a critical role in your advancement at work.

Talk About Your Accomplishments

Formal performance discussions (hopefully) provide you with an opportunity to share how you contributed to the organization over the last year. While these conversations can be incredibly beneficial, it's time to get comfortable talking about your projects and outcomes the other 364 days of the year. There is an art to graciously sharing your accomplishments, and it involves being authentic in your pride, your motivations, and your timing.

You can begin to infuse updates about your contributions into everyday conversations. For example, when you find yourself in a Zoom meeting with the big boss before others join or ride the elevator with a more senior leader and they ask, "How are you?" In either situation, instead of the usual "Great, thanks," try this, "I am working on/recently completed [*project name*] and we learned [*brief outcome*]." It makes for a much more engaging conversation, and you highlight what you've been working on.

From there, you can work your way up to sharing your expertise with larger audiences by teaching a "lunch and learn" at your office, presenting an overview of your work at a town hall or team meeting, or even volunteering to lead a cross-functional team project.

Send an NNTR Update

As important as it is for all senior leaders in your office to be aware of your strengths, you should focus on building this aspect of the relationship with your boss specifically. One of my go-to strategies to communicate your contributions clearly and consistently with your boss is the NNTR Update—as in "No Need to Respond." This is an email update you send to your boss once or twice a week to share on your own terms the priorities you're working on and what you've accomplished. When you can't necessarily have a water cooler conversation or stop by the boss's office, it's a chance for you to maintain contact and stay visible.

You can use this approach in multiple ways: send a note to share updates, vocalize your priorities and everything you have on your plate for that week, or ask questions about a challenge you're having. This is helpful for both you and your boss to have a reference of what has happened each week, which will be valuable for performance evaluation conversations or asking for a raise or promotion later on.

Plus, by labeling this email NNTR, you free your boss from any need to reply while still doing your part to advocate for yourself and manage up. (That being said, I do hope you're working in a place where you feel supported and valued with or without these emails.)

If you want to put this NNTR Update into practice, you can use the following template:

Monday's Subject Line: NNTR Update

Dear Boss:

Here's what I am working on this week: [*project X, project Y, and project Z*]. If there's anything you'd like me to change or add, I welcome your feedback.

Have a great week.

[*Your Name*]

When possible, be sure to include anyone you have collaborated with, any big meetings you have, or even something you're excited about.

Friday's Subject Line: Weekly Update

Dear Boss:

Here are all the things I was able to accomplish this week: project X and project Y. I am still working on project Z and will continue the related work next week. Look forward to sharing more then.

Have a great weekend.

[*Your Name*]

You can and should personalize these templates so they suit your communication style and your boss's. For example, these updates can happen on a monthly basis instead of a weekly basis.

NAVIGATE WORKPLACE CHALLENGES

When you think about leading from where you are, it's also important to understand how to navigate different factors that can work against even your best efforts. Let's walk through a few of the most common challenges you may face today.

Office Politics

Understanding the structures and systems in the workplace environment requires political savvy, often referred to as office politics. I hear many people, particularly women, say they don't like to play office politics. I understand why, but here's the thing: if you're not playing the game, someone else will be. So, instead of pushing the concept of office politics to the side and thinking of it as petty gossip and whispering behind each other's backs, it's time to reframe our thinking and see this part of the job for what it really is.

Office politics means understanding organizational dynamics, the way you influence the people around you, and how you advocate for yourself to get what you and your team need. When you reframe office politics this way, it becomes much more accessible—and important—because not being involved can lead to missed opportunities to advance your career. There are ways to be conscious of office politics and to help them work for you, without selling your soul, so let's walk through the steps.

Step 1: Understand How the Organization Works
Before you start to "play politics," develop an understanding of how your organization operates, including who holds power and how ideas are shared. You can get a sense of this from listening in internal meetings and observing interactions. If you have a trusting relationship with your boss, you can ask them who the decision makers are in other departments so you can be aware. Also keep an eye out for who gets promoted and which departments they're in. All of these will factor into your plan of how to navigate the organization.

Step 2: Make Genuine, Proactive Connections
Once you have a sense of the way things are done, it is important to start to proactively connect with the influential people in your organization. This means building genuine relationships, taking a real interest in other people's projects and roles, and getting to know the people you work with—directly or indirectly—in a deeper way. You also want them to know who you are and want to support you.

As you build these connections, you will form a better understanding of how people work and what motivates them. You'll also get a broader view on the organizational culture—and you might even make some new office friendships.

A word of caution: it's as important to foster some kind of relationship with the people in the office whom you don't necessarily get along with but who could (negatively) affect your work, too. Think of it as a "strategic alliance," which you need to thoughtfully invest in to achieve your goals.

Step 3: Put Politics to Work for You
Now it's time to put politics to work for you. This means being clear on your goals *and* the organization's goals and putting your influence and expertise to work in order to achieve both. It also

means being aware that you will have to rise above the things (or people) that might get in the way and focus on how to move the work forward, rather than let others drag you down. Along the way, do not lose sight of the importance of proudly sharing what you've accomplished.

You see, even when your projects have been successful, the real work is just as much about speaking up for yourself and telling people about your results and effort. When I missed the mark on understanding office politics earlier in my career, I vowed I wouldn't make this mistake again and I would help coach other women to be better prepared.

You owe it to yourself to learn about the politics in your organization and how to navigate them, even if it feels uncomfortable. I get it. I was taught that there are three things you don't talk about at work: religion, money, and politics. I know that kind of politics is different than what we're talking about, but these unwritten rules are part of what hold women back in their careers. So the next time you question whether to share about your work or use your influence for yourself, remember what could be lost if you don't.

Bias at Work

Bias at work results in making quick judgments about people based on their personal experiences and cultural background—and unfortunately, it happens every day. Clients and friends share with me that they've heard comments about their race, ethnicity, gender, age, weight, and pregnancy status from potential hiring managers, colleagues, and others. I've personally experienced bias at work, too.

No one should ever be devalued or disrespected for being who they are. If you do experience bias at work or are concerned about it being an issue at some point, I suggest the following:

- **Find a network.** Connect with other colleagues who can relate to and understand your perspective, which will help reaffirm your role and belonging in the organization. You may find this community with an internal employee resource group (ERG) or an external professional development association. Don't have one of these communities you can connect with? Start one. It will be a wonderful leadership opportunity for you and a welcomed resource for others.
- **Watch your language.** Your own language matters and can contribute to reducing bias in the workplace. Practice saying people's names correctly as a way to honor who they are. To avoid ageism in the workplace, remove the words "young" and "old" from your work vocabulary. One way to start doing this when you catch yourself is to say, "early career" or "late career."
- **Talk to your manager.** If you're experiencing bias at work, thoughtfully approach your manager about what you've been dealing with. Be prepared to give specific examples. It's possible your manager isn't aware of the situation, as they may be working to disrupt their own biases, too. If you were passed over for a project or assignment, see if you can get more insights on what your manager wants you to do differently. When you're having conversations like this, keep documentation (your own notes or emails). Though I hope it doesn't come to involving HR or legal ramifications, it's always a good idea to keep track of things.

No matter what point in your career you're in, it's important to be aware of the role bias can unintentionally play at work. Ultimately, organizations are strongest when we have diverse perspectives and backgrounds at the table, and we still have work to do to get our workplaces to where they need to be.

• • •

You add value to your organization through the experience and energy you bring, whether you've been working for 2 years or 20. Lead yourself accordingly.

Leading from where you are is more than an opportunity—it's your responsibility. Stop waiting for a magical moment to be a leader, and apply what you've learned here in this chapter. Your time to lead (with or without a title) is now.

BOLD MOVES TO MAKE NOW

Make a list of three things you will begin doing now to lead from where you are—and use at least one at work this week.

Send an unprompted note to your manager sharing about a work accomplishment or progress you've made on an important project—with a focus on communicating your value.

Consider the organizational politics where you work and identify one way you can build your influence.

Grow as a Leader

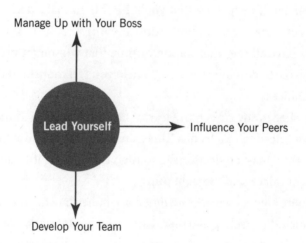

Manage Up with Your Boss

Lead Yourself → Influence Your Peers

Develop Your Team

As important as it is for you to lead from where you are, there are even more significant expectations for your leadership when you formally manage people. In addition to leading yourself, you'll also need to manage up with your boss, influence your peers, and develop your team (see figure).

Leading yourself and others means you'll be pulled in different directions and faced with difficult situations. In those hard moments, you'll need to be clear on your "why" as a leader so you can be prepared to bring the best of you to your leadership. This chapter outlines the different ways you'll be expected to lead yourself and others, including decision-making strategies, managing former peers, supporting team members' growth by giving feedback, and developing a strong relationship with your boss.

Whether you're new to management or have been doing this for a while, this chapter will help you develop as a leader and continue to achieve your organizational outcomes.

DECISION-MAKING STRATEGIES FOR ANY SITUATION

As a leader, it's expected that you'll be able to make decisions to keep your team and organization moving forward. You won't always have all the information or time that you might prefer, so you'll have to develop strategies to help you feel more confident in your choices.

Earlier in my career, my fear of failure undermined the confidence I needed as a leader. This translated into spending far too much time making decisions and then ruminating if I had made the right call or said the right thing.

There are many reasons women might hesitate to make a decision, including feeling like there isn't enough information or there's too much information. You could also be dealing with decision fatigue or fear of failure. In my experience of leading large teams in complex organizations, coaching leaders at all levels, and running a business, I've learned you have to make the decisions anyway.

It's not overdramatizing to worry about being wrong. Research shows that women are penalized more harshly than men when they make a wrong decision. In one study by Victoria Brescoll at Yale School of Management, women were consistently judged by their failures, even when they received positive evaluations for their leadership.[1]

Knowing that your judgment will be questioned and evaluated, often unfairly, it's no wonder you may experience more hesitation about making decisions! Society has work to do to reduce the double bind on women in leadership, and it's essential for men to perceive women as strong decision makers and leaders. As we continue to work toward both, here are six strategies you can use to strengthen and reinforce your decision-making skills as a woman leader.

Coach Yourself as You Would a Friend

According to a 2013 research study of women corporate board directors, they tended to engage in more collaboration and consensus-building for their decision-making.[2] Based on this finding, one way to improve your decision-making process could be to simulate the experience of discussing with others. For example, talk to yourself as you would coach someone else. What would you advise your best friend or close colleague to do? When you focus on how you would counsel others, you give yourself a bit of distance from the decision at hand, and it could be just enough to see things more clearly. You tend to be harder on your own decisions than you are on others. Because this approach misses the opportunity to increase buy-in from stakeholders, it will be important to clearly communicate your decision to others after it's been made.

Create More Options

Oftentimes, you unintentionally limit your options when making decisions because you think there is only one right option. Try to find ways to create more options for yourself to bring an abundance mindset and your best thinking to the situation.

If your first option isn't available or possible, acknowledge it and move on. Ask yourself, "What is my next best option right now?" You'll help reframe your decision in the context of the moment you're in.

It's also important to realize that binary decision-making, which is the idea that there should be one of two options (Option A or Option B), can limit your thinking. In Therese Huston's book *How Women Decide*, she suggests that even when you think the scenario has two options, it's likely you've reduced your decision into either yes or no. So, make sure to have three options when fully considering a decision. A third potential option may not occur to you right away, but stretch yourself to consider what else could be possible. My favorite choice is often Option C!

Prepare for Mistakes

Avoiding all mistakes is not a feasible leadership strategy, nor should it be your goal—but it was how I operated for much of my early career. It seemed like the best way to succeed in my position, or at the minimum, to avoid negative feedback. But by recognizing that at some point everyone will make a mistake or fail, you can instead focus on building resilience. It's not the falling, but rather the getting back up (which often makes you more determined and focused on learning) that will support you in advancing as a leader.

Acknowledge the Role of Emotions

Emotional contagion is when you pass on your emotions, knowingly or unknowingly, to other people. Sigal Barsade of the

Wharton School extensively studied this concept, and she discovered that your emotions affect your decision-making—and those around you.[3] Though it makes sense that your feelings influence how you see the world, most people are unaware in the moment of the significant role emotions play (or what their exact feelings are, for that matter). Now that you *do* have this awareness, start paying more attention to the role of your emotions not just to benefit those around you, but to benefit your own judgment, too. A few ways you can reduce negative emotional contagion include:

1. **Take time to reset.** After every meeting, give yourself 10 seconds to breathe deeply and reset yourself for the next meeting. It's also especially helpful to reset when you're working remotely and you transition from a work mindset to home mindset or vice versa.

2. **Acknowledge your feelings when something difficult happens.** Name the emotion and be specific. Tell yourself, "I feel anxious or upset" rather than "I am anxious or upset" and remind yourself the feeling won't last.

3. **Develop a plan.** You might say, "I feel anxious about this upcoming meeting. To help me get through this, I am going to review my notes again and then listen to music." If you're around your team members or family members, share this plan with them so they can support you—and learn from your strategies about how to work through emotions.

4. **Practice active listening.** The more you focus on being present in the moment, the harder it is to overanalyze what happened to you in the past.

5. **Engage in activities that remind you of your optimism.** This might mean turning to gratitude, doing something kind for someone else, or reaching out to others.

You can't always avoid getting upset when things happen, but you can increase your self-awareness of your emotions and, as a result, regulate your decision-making.

Consider the Short- and Long-Term Outcomes

When making a big decision, consider both the short- and long-term outcomes. To put things into perspective, ask yourself, "Will delaying or changing the decision make things significantly better?" Having the qualifier will help you consider whether you truly need to gather more information or evaluate other possibilities. If it won't make things significantly better, proceed and focus on making progress rather than making it perfect. Even incremental progress is worth celebrating. There is rarely a perfect decision anyway! You have to take the risk in order to innovate.

Take the First Step

Sometimes the most important decision is to take the first step. My mantra might help you with this: you're making the best decision you can with the information you have at the time. I find this reassuring, because you can change course in the future if you have new information that suggests going in a different direction.

Though much of the same advice offered to women about decision-making could also apply to men, the experiences women have in the workplace suggest a more nuanced approach. Women will be evaluated more negatively for their leadership solely on the basis of gender (ugh!), so it's not just your decisions, but the way people perceive your decisions.

In my own career, I decided to focus more on being respected than being liked. I did this by acknowledging the value I bring to the organization instead of waiting for others to validate me. I chose to remain focused on how to best serve others, even when it was hard or sometimes unpopular. I also learned to listen to my intuition again, which has always guided me in making big decisions. The answers were there because I had the experience to back them up, but I had stopped hearing them through the noise of everyone else's opinions.

Becoming a stronger, more confident decision-maker didn't happen overnight. Instead, I learned over time how to manage ambiguity, balance data and intuition, and harness my emotions. I also practiced decision-making to make informed choices with less effort. And I gave myself grace to learn from my decisions, even the "wrong" ones.

The role of a leader is to keep moving things forward, making the best decisions you can on behalf of the team and organization, with the information you have.

FROM PEER TO SUPERVISOR

As you advance in your career, especially if you're able to grow within the same organization, it's likely that you'll experience managing people who were formerly your peers. They may have even been your friends.

I lived this: in my first big management role, I went—overnight—from being the friend you went out for margaritas with, to being the boss who did your performance evaluations. It was one of the biggest professional challenges I've experienced—even though I tried to prepare for this.

You see, throughout the interview process for this promotion, I was asked the same question over and over: "How will you handle the transition from peer to manager?" I had anticipated this question, as I was preparing to go from individual contributor to my first significant role managing people, and I would remain within the same team. I shared my thoughtfully planned and practiced answers during the interviews and, fortunately, got the job.

In the weeks leading up to the new role, I read every book and article on this topic, attended multiple seminars, and talked to mentors and trusted advisors. All of the advice made it sound like it might be difficult at first, but it would go smoothly eventually. In the first week, I realized none of the advice or learning truly prepared me for going from peer to supervisor.

When I first started out as a manager, I mistakenly thought I could keep doing everything I had done as a superstar employee, but perhaps better, and that would be the key to leadership. After all, most people are tapped for management roles as recognition for what they did well as individual performers.

I ended up doing everything myself, though—which meant I didn't bring my team along with me and left me feeling burnt out and alone. And this led me to realize the first and most important lesson for new managers: your job is not to be the superstar anymore. Now your job is to support your team. The reason a team exists is to accomplish more than any individual could on their own.

Here's what I would do differently and how you can be intentional with your immediate next steps in order to have a successful transition from peer to supervisor. (Many of these things will help every manager, not only those who are going from peer to supervisor.)

Acknowledge the Transition

Make time to meet with each direct report individually with the purpose of establishing your new boss / team member relationship. During this meeting, ask them what they enjoy most about their work and how you can help them thrive in their role. You can share your leadership style and open a dialogue regarding any questions or concerns they may have.

Your transition into a management role will likely be as uncomfortable for you as it is for your team members, so go ahead and acknowledge this instead of pretending it doesn't exist.

As part of your new role, things at work will have to change, and you may have mixed feelings about this. It's okay to feel sad about missing out on your friendships while also being excited about what is ahead for your career.

Create a Distinction in Your New Role

You'll want to clearly define the new boundaries that will exist in your relationship. This means you can't be there to sit and listen while your team member talks through every step of a project like you might have before. To create a distinction in your new role as the boss, remind team members that you believe in their abilities, are available as a resource, and look forward to project updates in your next one-on-one meeting. This also means your team members shouldn't drop by your office to share the latest company gossip, but you do want them to feel comfortable raising concerns about things happening in the organization.

As I worked through my leadership transition to manager, I had to learn the difference in the impact of what I said when I was in a position of authority, even if my intent was the same as when I was a colleague. When you're the boss, your feedback carries more weight. One of my favorite descriptions of this is that a boss's whisper can sound like a shout.[4] For example, you may have been the go-to editor for your friend's important work emails, and it can be interpreted differently when you mark up their documents as the boss.

Before you offer feedback, consider if you've laid the groundwork for this to be productive for both of you, such as rebuilding trust and clarifying new roles. You can also remind them you're here to support them (which, of course, you also did as a friend, but now it is part of what's expected of you as their boss). Then be specific about what needs to be improved and actionable steps to do so.

For example, "I've always admired your consistency and clarity in your reports. The last few reports haven't reflected the level of analysis needed. What can I do to best support you in getting back on track?"

Make a point to proactively tell your team members specifically about what they do well, too. This type of feedback from a boss is also amplified when received by a team member. It's where your whisper-turned-shout factor can make a positive difference!

Maintaining (or Not Maintaining) Work Friendships

The perspectives are mixed on whether you should thoughtfully maintain work friendships with direct reports or keep the boss/subordinate roles separate. I struggled with this in my first peer to manager transition.

I attempted to do a hybrid version where I would announce which "hat" I was wearing when talking to a team member ("boss" or "friend"). The idea was that I could still maintain at least part of the friendship in certain circumstances. But this meant I was switching back and forth frequently, sometimes in the middle of a single conversation, and got lost on which hat I was wearing when. I learned quickly that this strategy wasn't going to work, and I decided it would be clearer to have only professional relationships with my former peers.

But it wasn't easy.

The first time I saw the team heading out for cocktails after a work event, I felt left out because I wasn't invited, even though I knew that would eventually happen. It still hurt because I had been included in those invitations just a few months prior.

One more lesson of leadership is that your choices and actions are being watched. So if you choose to remain friends with your direct reports, the responsibility is on you to treat all of your team members equitably. You wouldn't want to be seen as playing favorites with select team members.

As I've developed as a leader, I've found my position on work friendships has evolved. Like all relationships, it takes trust, communication, and compassion.

Provide Vision and Clarity (Not Answers and Solutions)

I had always prided myself on being the friend and colleague who supported others, whether serving as a trusted resource for questions about work, being counted on for coffee breaks and peer mentoring, or putting out work fires. The difference as a manager is that you can't answer everyone's questions all the time (nor should you), and your role is to clarify the work for others, not do it all yourself. I had to learn that sharing my expertise as a manager was often less valuable than encouraging others to find the answers within or for themselves. I also learned the hard way that it's my job to coach them to solve their problems and manage difficult situations, not necessarily do it for them.

During a conversation with a mentor about some of my challenges as a leader, she reminded me that my focus should be vision and clarity (versus answers and solutions). She recommended that I needed to stop "taking on the monkey," a phrase popularized by a *Harvard Business Review* article from the 1970s that is still relevant today.[5] In corporate speak, this happens when your team members put their work problems onto you: hence you take the monkey on your back.

You can break this habit by helping draw out your team members' thinking instead of giving your opinion first. For example, try asking your team member questions like "What factors are you weighing in making this decision?" "What do you think the next step should be?" or "How should we handle this challenge?" Asking them their thoughts helps you build buy-in and shows you value their perspective.

Remember: the leader's role is not to solve problems, but to help their team become better problem-solvers.

Ask for Help

During this transition, one of the things I missed most was having someone to help guide me through so many difficult decisions and situations. What I should have done was reached out to my boss and asked for help, but I didn't because I mistakenly thought that would be a sign of weakness or failure in my new role. Asking for help means that you still have more to learn, but it doesn't invalidate the experience you already have. I hope that you respect your boss as a leader and can count on them for insights. If not, I recommend finding an established colleague in your field you can turn to when you need guidance.

I eventually worked with an executive coach to support my leadership development, and she helped me see what was holding me back, both in my organization and in myself. Together we developed a plan for the areas I wanted to work on—and what I could control. She reminded me what my strengths and values were and showed me how to leverage them differently. It was a life- and career-changing experience that I highly recommend, if you have a chance to participate.

I've since left the organization where I had my first big management role, but the memories of what I wish I had done differently haven't left me. When you move on, make sure you take the learning with you. Better yet, share that learning with others. In turn, you'll be able to make meaning from your experiences.

All leadership transitions are difficult. I was so busy trying to do what everyone else suggested I do that I forgot what made me a great colleague or friend in the first place—caring about team members as people.

GET BETTER AT GIVING FEEDBACK

Giving effective feedback will be one of the most consequential parts of your job as a leader, because it's how you can contribute to your team members' growth.

I wasn't always comfortable giving feedback. Earlier in my career as a manager, I vacillated between wanting people to like me and feeling like I needed to assert my authority. This meant I either shied away from saying anything that would upset team members or went in the total opposite direction and told it like it was without considering how the other person would receive it. Neither worked.

It took me a long time to learn how my feedback could support team members' growth if delivered in a way that focused on building relationships. Once I did, I understood that it is possible to be direct and compassionate at the same time.

To be a great leader, you'll need to get comfortable communicating compassionately and clearly with your team members because you genuinely believe in their potential and care about their growth. Here's how to start.

Include Feedback as a Team Value

Have ongoing discussions about the importance of feedback, beginning with onboarding new staff and continuing throughout their tenure. Effective feedback has to be built on trust and psychological safety, which allows team members to feel safe at work. When someone feels this way in the office, they know they can speak up and share their thoughts without negative repercussions, and they can take risks to innovate. It takes intention and trust to build this kind of work environment, so be sure to openly talk about feedback in the context of learning and innovation to create understanding of expectations. This should happen well before delivering any actual feedback and isn't meant to be used only in performance evaluations.

Another way to ensure that feedback is a part of your team culture is to provide coaching for all managers on the team about how to give feedback and encourage them to coach each other, too. And you should expect and encourage feedback from your team to you, too. In the same way your feedback should help your team members grow, you will also grow from understanding what your team needs from you as a leader. Work hard to create an environment where it's possible for staff to speak up.

Structure Your Feedback

When you deliver feedback, first reaffirm that you care about your team member's growth. Then be specific about what behaviors you want them to continue doing (reinforcing feedback) or what behaviors you want them to stop doing (redirecting feedback) and actionable steps to do so.

EXAMPLES OF REINFORCING FEEDBACK

I really appreciate when you turn your materials in by deadline.

I'd like to see you do more of the budget analysis in order to achieve our financial outcomes next quarter.

In these examples, I indicated what a team member already does well or what they could do more of, so they have a clearer understanding of what they should continue to do to be successful in their role. I also made a point to connect their efforts to the organization's goals, so they can see how they contribute to the broader organizational outcomes.

EXAMPLE OF REDIRECTING FEEDBACK

You have missed a few deadlines on this project. What's contributing to that? When you miss deadlines, you also affect your team members as they are relying on you to complete your section to finalize this project. If you anticipate missing a deadline in the future, please tell me as far in advance as possible, so we can determine what to do.

In this example, I stated what I saw happening, asked questions to show I care about them and want to know more about their workload, and shared how this behavior affects others. I also clarified what my expectations are, so the team member understands what to do in a situation like this and knows I'm there as a resource and partner.

You may also find ways to help employees reflect on their own strengths and growth areas by asking questions, instead of only sharing your perceptions. For example, instead of immediately sharing your thoughts on a meeting, ask, "How do you feel that meeting went?" If there was something you noticed they could have done differently in advance of the meeting, you could certainly state what you think, or you could dig a little deeper to understand by asking, "What was your process to prepare?" The more you can get past the surface to understand a team member's motivations, values, or processes, the better you'll be able to support them. The more they can see the learning moment for themselves, the likelier they'll be to change behaviors.

Time Your Feedback

Consider appropriate timing and place for feedback, but don't overthink it. I don't believe in offering feedback in front of other people (unless a team member is doing something to negatively affect someone else in a way that requires addressing immediately). Instead, find a time and place where you and the team member can speak privately.

Be sure to account for a team member's frame of mind, such as if a team member has a lot going on outside of the office that could be affecting their performance, and try to give some space and grace, so your feedback can be heard. You might ask them, "Does this feel like a good time to talk through some things I am noticing?"

If they react poorly and ask to wait until the next day, respect this. You don't, however, need to wait for a formal one-on-one meeting, especially if it's a week or two away, because it might be hard to remember pertinent details with so much time in between. Also, if there is something time-sensitive that you need to share with your team member, you don't need to ask permission.

I coach managers on my team and clients to give what I call "flash feedback," for example, directly following a meeting, so the person doesn't forget the circumstances and can benefit from learning in the moment. Plus, when team members know feedback is a value, this is something they will be prepared to hear.

Remember to Give Positive Feedback, Too

Feedback tends to get a negative reputation because it can refer to something that needs to be improved. Remember the importance of positive feedback, too! When offering praise or recognition, center it on the other person. Specifically acknowledge the achievement so your team member knows what they did well and what to repeat in the future. Praise the person's efforts and how it helps the organization (not how it benefits you). Research shows that this increases the likelihood of positive emotions for the feedback recipient—and builds relationships.[6]

Offer positive feedback genuinely and authentically (people can tell when it's not) and more frequently than you might think is necessary. In a hybrid work environment when your team members may feel more disconnected from their work and each other, this encouragement is especially meaningful.

MANAGE UP WITH YOUR BOSS

Developing a positive relationship with your boss is imperative. It can define how you feel about your job—and affect how your boss views your work.

But it's a balance. You want your boss to trust you and support you, but you don't want to compromise who you are to achieve that. You want to be someone they can count on, but you don't want to be the yes-woman for everything either. So, what can you do to set yourself up for success?

"Managing up" is the common term for knowing how to work well with your boss. Here's what it's not: sucking up. And it's most definitely not manipulative. Rather, it's about opening the lines of communication, and it benefits both you and your boss.

Here are four things you can do to develop a strong relationship with your boss:

Learn Your Boss's Expectations and Style

You can learn your boss's leadership style by observing and listening. You can also ask questions about what kind of communication works well for your boss, how they approach their work, and what they value. Then follow through accordingly.

If they want to be copied on every email, keep them included. If they prefer brevity, focus on speaking succinctly. It's beneficial for you to share with your boss about your own style and how they can best support you, too.

Understand What Matters to Your Boss

You will need to understand what your boss's priorities are and how they align with yours. Then it's your job to connect the dots to help advance those projects. I like to get a sense of what keeps my boss up at night, because my goal is to solve for what's valuable to the organization (and help them sleep!).

Over time, figure out ways to anticipate your boss's needs and offer to be helpful. Here's how to put this in action: ask your boss, "What can I take off your plate?" This shows your genuine interest in supporting them and gives you access to higher-level projects. Time this strategically, so you don't burn yourself out, such as before they go on vacation or if they seem particularly overwhelmed. This is a way to stretch yourself and move things forward for your boss—and it has worked for me to advance my career.

Give Feedback to Your Boss

It can be challenging to know how to disagree with your boss, but keep in mind that a good boss will have hired you because they value and respect your perspective and input—both of which are necessary to advance the organization and support them. Figuring out how to effectively give feedback to your boss is an essential component of building trust with them.

Take some time to reflect on appropriate timing and be clear on what your goals are before approaching your boss to share your thoughts. You might even ask your boss if they'd be open to you sharing an alternate perspective. This gives a signal that you might be sharing something your boss isn't expecting and gives buy-in for you to proceed.

The goal is to make it comfortable for your boss to listen thoughtfully to your perspective. Stay focused on the situation, not your perception, judgment, or the story you may be telling yourself. Be confident in delivering your message, but humble in your delivery. I recommend that you also affirm your boss's authority. I like to use phrases like "I defer to you on this," "I welcome your expertise," or "Thank you for the chance to share this perspective" in these situations.

Connect with Your Boss as a Person

When you're feeling disconnected from your boss or frustrated with how they're handling something, it helps to remember that your boss is human and approach them with empathy. Keep in mind that your boss has many competing priorities and is likely experiencing their own learning and challenges.

Try connecting with your boss on a personal level. Your goal is to better understand who they are, not to be best friends. In a casual conversation, ask about their weekend or what hobbies they have. In a one-on-one meeting, ask them to share a story about their career and what helped them be successful or what they wish they had done differently. If you're able to see your boss as a whole person—in some ways, just like you—it can help you relate to them and ease some of the work frustrations you have.

Building a positive relationship with your boss is a critical skill to your success in a work environment. Find ways to understand how your boss's goals and yours align and then work toward those outcomes—together.

. . .

Leading yourself and others is a significant responsibility. Here's the thing that no one ever told me, but I learned over time: leadership is one of the most rewarding and challenging things you can do at work. When you commit to serving and supporting others in being the best version of themselves, you truly have the power to change lives—including your own.

BOLD MOVES TO MAKE NOW

Write down what motivates you to lead people and one thing you want to be known for as a leader.

Choose one decision-making strategy you will try this week when you're feeling stuck.

Practice communicating with compassionate directness in a feedback conversation or in asking for what you want.

Be the Boss Everyone Wants to Work For

Who is the best boss you ever had? What made this person the best boss? I've been fortunate to work for many amazing leaders throughout my career, and I've learned from all of them about the kind of leader I wanted to be. I've also worked for not-so-great bosses who made my work life very difficult, and, well, I've learned from them, too.

Many leaders believe their role is to mold their team members into what the organization wants. Or worse, into mini versions of them. This will only get you so far.

It's an incredible privilege to lead people, to be responsible for developing future leaders. My goal as a boss is to support employees in being the best version of themselves (as defined by them) and help them reach their potential. As a leader, I want to bring out the strengths already within my team members and help them live their why.

This doesn't mean I've always been the best boss. Despite my best efforts, I have unintentionally shut down conversations or rushed people along. I've held back on feedback because I didn't want to hurt someone's feelings, which ended up becoming a bigger deal later. All of that to say, being the best boss doesn't mean being perfect. It means continuing to show up as the best leader you can be, because you want to serve others. Sure, it takes extra effort to understand what people need from you as a leader; help them feel valued; communicate what's on your heart, even through uncertainty; and be truly inclusive. And when your team thrives, you'll know it's all worth it.

YOUR "ABOUT ME" DOCUMENT AND USER MANUAL

As I transitioned into a leadership role, I read about and reflected on the kind of leader and colleague I wanted to be. Around that same time, I came across an article that explained the concept of a User Manual, which is really just a description of the best way to work with someone.[1] The piece, written by Abby Falik, founder and CEO of Global Citizen Year, who learned about the concept from an article by Adam Bryant, the former "Corner Office" columnist for the *New York Times*,[2] really resonated with me, as I wanted to help my new team understand who I am and how I approach my work, so we could build trust faster and I could learn how to best support them.

After reflecting on Falik's post, I spent time writing my own thoughts about my leadership style and values, and I sought input from others on what they wished they had known about me earlier on. From there, I developed what I call an "About Me" document, which I shared with my new team in a group meeting in my first week on the job. Since that meeting, it's become a foundational part of my leadership approach.

Creating your own About Me document can build trust and clarity with a new team or with a team you've worked with for a long time, particularly as a reset in the remote/hybrid world. Don't take for granted that you know each other at work. Ask people to tell their own story.

Here are six parts to the About Me document and prompts that will help you create your own.

My Leadership Approach

How would you describe your work or leadership approach? You may want to include your expectations of yourself and your team.

These are a few of my personal notes:

- I commit to creating a work environment where you can bring your whole self to work.
- I align with the model of compassionate directness.[3]
- I believe in celebrating progress.

My Leadership Philosophy

Tell your team what is important to you: your values reflect who you are. Think about the experiences and aspirations that define you. If you spent time crafting your why statement in Chapter 3, your team will benefit from knowing this, as it illustrates your motivation and purpose. Some examples of my philosophy include:

- Family comes first. You define what family means to you, whether that's a partner, children, parents, siblings, friends, or pets.

- How to be successful at work: lead from where you are.
- Trust is given on day one; it does not have to be earned with me. It can, however, be broken and is hard to rebuild.
- I believe in being competitive with yourself and not with others.
- I believe that success is everyone's responsibility.

And, finally, my why:

- *To help others achieve more than they thought possible, so that they can fulfill their potential and find joy.*

You Get the Best of Me When . . .

Are you a morning person, or do you need two cups of coffee before you start your workday? Do you prefer to make decisions in hallway conversations or formal meetings? Be clear on what works best for you, so your team can maximize their interactions and time with you.

People get the best of me when . . .

- They don't ask for 2 minutes and then take 10 minutes. I value my time and theirs, so it helps when someone says, "I would like to get your thoughts before I present at that meeting later this week" rather than asking for two minutes without a topic.
- Show me your thinking. I like to understand where people are coming from in their planning and decision-making when I'm serving as a resource.

How Best to Communicate with Me

Everyone has a preferred way of communicating. Clearly indicate what works best for you, so your team doesn't have to guess. (Hint: they will probably guess incorrectly.)

My preferences are:

- Face-to-face over everything, and texting is a close second to keep me informed or to get a faster response in a time-sensitive situation.
- In an email or document, put the ask or most important information up front.

How to Help Me

Are you the kind of boss who needs data or relies on intuition? Are you someone who wants the full story or just the synopsis? Let your team know what you need to be successful.

I prefer:

- If a project or task takes longer than expected, overcommunicate where you are in the process—even if there's no action needed on my part—so I don't have to wonder where things are. I call it the "non-update update." I make a commitment to provide this to others, too.
- If you're unsure what I mean, please ask for clarification rather than guessing or trying to figure it out on your own. I'm not always as clear as I want to be, and I want to set you up for success.

What People Misunderstand About Me

Your authority amplifies your actions. Everything you do or say as a leader is being watched by your team. Furthermore, there may be something that worked for you as an individual contributor that doesn't translate the same way now that you are a manager. For example: You may like to ask a lot of questions during a conversation, which helps you learn about a topic. However, your team members could interpret that you don't trust their decisions—that's the sort of information you'd share here.

For me, this shows up when . . .

- I speak with passion and conviction. This can come across as if I don't want to hear feedback. In reality, I'm open to other ideas and willing to change my mind.

Telling my team up front that my style can be misunderstood minimizes uncertainty about my intentions. It also clarifies that I want team members to offer their thinking and to be a partner in holding me accountable.

- I move and think quickly, and I don't expect you to do things exactly the way I do. It can be challenging for team members to know how much autonomy they have in how to do the work. I try to overcommunicate my expectations.

And as a general rule, if you're the boss who often leaves it at "Can you talk?" or "Let's discuss," just don't. Those are some of the worst sentences a boss can ever say. Keep in mind that it's almost always misunderstood, and even an About Me clarification won't change that. Always add a second sentence explaining the nature of the discussion so your team members don't start packing up their offices.

• • •

Don't be afraid to show your personality when you write this document! You can include a favorite quote, your role models, or a visual. All of these prompts are only suggestions, so do whatever works best for you to help your team understand you best. This is your opportunity to help your team thrive under your leadership by understanding who you are and how to work with you.

Of course, the most successful working relationships are built on mutual respect and understanding, so ask your team members to fill out an About Me document as well. You can provide them with the same template you used and then create a time to meet and discuss. After all, great leaders share who they are *and* care about who their employees are, too.

VALUE YOUR EMPLOYEES

I shifted my weight from side to side as the all-staff meeting went longer than usual. I should definitely not have tried out my cute new heels on this particular day. What kept me going was that I had recently had a huge win at work, and sometimes team member successes were recognized at these group meetings. As the meeting ended, I realized my name wouldn't be called that day. I had gotten my hopes up unnecessarily. Again. Though I'd love to say I didn't rely on external recognition, it didn't mean I didn't value it—because it was how the organization showed it valued me.

When I finally got up the nerve to ask my manager about it, he looked surprised and told me I should learn to pat myself on the back. He went on to explain that he hadn't received any recognition earlier in his career, and it made him into the leader he was. I'm sure I looked as surprised as he did—although not for the reasons you might expect. I was taken aback because that wasn't the kind of leader I wanted to be for other people. A leader's role is to create a supportive work environment where employees feel valued and appreciated for their work and who they are. When your employees feel valued by you, it will create positive outcomes for all involved.

I suspect you've worked somewhere you didn't feel valued, too. This is your chance as a boss to change that for others. Here's what that can look like on a day-to-day basis at work.

Practice Gratitude at Work

Gratitude at work is more than saying thank you (although that's a great place to begin!). To effectively show gratitude to someone, be clear about what you appreciate about them, what they did, how they positively affected the organization or other people, and what can happen as a result of their efforts. When you use a structure like this, the person can understand what specifically they did well and the context of how it made a difference to others. Of course, whatever you say should reflect your genuine feelings about the person's efforts.

Here's what this can sound like in action: "Meg, your superpower is proactively anticipating what will be needed in a meeting, and the briefing you developed helped everyone be better prepared and resulted in a new gift."

You should also find ways to infuse gratitude into your workplace culture. Start your team meeting by asking everyone to write down three things they are grateful for and invite people to volunteer to share something from their list. Invite the team to share how a colleague helped them or supported them at work. If you're looking for something a bit more involved and special, our team organized an activity where we labeled a blank notebook with each team member's name and then passed them around for colleagues to write notes of gratitude about that person. This can be easily adapted for a remote/hybrid work environment, too.

Specific gratitude from a boss means "I see you" in a way that other praise can't. Employees want to be recognized for their contributions and most important, they want to be recognized for who they are as a person. Don't underestimate the power of a small, yet genuine compliment to a team member.

In case you need a little extra motivation to get started, here's my favorite stat ever on gratitude. In one study, Francesca Gino and Adam Grant, of Harvard Business School and the Wharton School, respectively, found that fundraising executives who received personal thanks from their manager for their efforts and contributions increased their outreach metrics by 50 percent.[4] *Fifty percent!* Employee recognition directly affects team members' motivation and how they feel about their jobs, so make this a priority as you lead your team.

Develop Personalized Learning Experiences

In order to create meaningful learning for your team members, first you have to understand what they value and where they want to grow. Some employees will be clear on what they're looking for, and others may need you to help them consider prospective opportunities. You can discuss this in a one-on-one conversation or ask them to fill out a questionnaire on their own. These questions will help you get started:

- Why do you do this job?
- What do you aspire to?
- What is something you want to learn more about this year?
- What are you curious about, or what would you like to explore further?

Then find ways to personalize learning experiences for your team members and make a formal plan with them for their professional development throughout the year. You and your team member may determine that they will benefit from attending a conference or certificate program. Perhaps they can get involved with professional or industry organizations that offer skill building and networking opportunities.

Don't overlook the opportunities within your organization either. Identify projects in your department or another that your team member can take on to get more experience in a specific area of interest. You may also sign them up for an internal mentoring program or connect them with a senior leader for a coffee conversation.

One of my love languages is introducing people in my network to each other. I don't do it for everyone, but it brings me joy to connect two people for personal and/or professional development. If you're open to sharing your network, this is a way to show your team members that you believe in them.

Prioritize Your Team

During conversations with managers on my team and as I work with clients, I often hear that it's challenging to balance their management responsibilities with their own work projects. I know how hard it is to have days of back-to-back meetings while trying to manage deadlines and your inbox. However, if you want to be a great leader, you'll need to prioritize your team members. I believe leading a team comes before anything else, even the bottom line. Your job is to help others achieve their goals, which is as much about making yourself available when they need help working through a challenging situation as carving out time on your calendar to drop them a note to wish them well on their upcoming presentation. It also means following through on what you committed to.

Team members observe your actions. They notice when you're responsive to their emails, when you take time to reach out about something other than work deadlines, and when you show up for them in the most difficult times in the organization and the world. If you're willing to sacrifice something for yourself in service to your team or organization, research shows this, in turn, increases their commitment to you and the organization.[5] Remember this the next time you feel pulled in many directions and a team member asks for your help. This "distraction" is your job as a leader of people. When you invest in your people, the results will come.

Celebrate with Your Team

Celebrating wins, no matter the size, shows appreciation to your team members, and it also builds connections and meaningful culture. Surprise your team members with personalized communications sharing your appreciation. I've loved recording "happy anniversary" and "congratulations" personalized videos for team members and leaving unexpected notes of encouragement on their desks.

Create celebration rituals for your team or company to reinforce the value of community. A client shared with me that they shake maracas every time they close a sale. What a celebratory sound! One of my favorite work memories was dreaming up and implementing a New Year's Eve party (with party hats and confetti) *in June* to honor all of the work that went into a successful fundraising year. You could adapt this for your company's founder's day or another significant date.

Make wins part of your everyday work culture. I created the concept of Win of the Day (WOTD) to encourage my team to share wins with each other. Here's how it works: When you experience a win, you send an email, text, or Slack message to your team with WOTD as the headline. The win is defined by you: it could be that you received a response to a cold call, moved a project forward, or received a note of recognition. Once one person shares what she accomplished, her colleagues cheer her on, and you can see instantly how this can build confidence and culture. Also be sure when choosing a WOTD that you acknowledge progress, not just outcomes. The whole point of WOTD is to celebrate and remind each other that we're in this together. Because who couldn't use a little more joy at work?

COMMUNICATE COURAGEOUSLY AND COMPASSIONATELY

As a leader, your communication sets the tone for how your team feels about their work and you. They'll look to you as an example, so communicate consistently, transparently, and authentically every day—and especially in challenging times. It will be as much about what you say as what you don't say. It's also about how you create space for your team to speak up, too. Communicating courageously and compassionately means being willing to have the difficult conversation while leading with your heart. You won't always get it right, and that's okay. Stay focused on serving others and showing up for them and for you. Here's what this looks like in action.

Ask Open-Ended Questions

You've likely been put into your manager role because you have experience in your industry. Beyond your experience, you likely exceeded expectations in your role and were the go-to for your colleagues when they needed advice. Now that you're a leader, your role is to coach your team members to figure out the answers, rather than telling them what you would do. Practice asking open-ended questions (questions that start with *how, what, when*) to get them to share their perspective.

For example, instead of saying, "I've created a new process to help you streamline your work," try saying, "How can we develop a new process together to streamline our work outcomes?"

This isn't about asking questions simply to have a dialogue; it's to genuinely learn from and with your team. After all, as the amazing leader you are, you've hired people who are also amazing. You'll learn more about the team member's thinking, and you can create better and stronger ideas together. You might even be surprised to learn something new about them as a person. Plus, when they feel you're listening and acting on their ideas and caring about their perspective, this will help them feel valued at work.

My go-to phrase for open-ended dialogue: *Tell me more about that.*

Use Collaborative Language ("Yes, And")

How many times have you heard someone (maybe even yourself) say, "I totally agree with you, but . . . ."

Spoiler alert: that person does not totally agree with you.

As kind human beings, we want to sound supportive even when we're really not, so we say things like that, even though it doesn't make sense. No wonder we start to wonder who really supports us!

You can have a supportive conversation with someone else and open up the dialogue to more possibilities. This is where "Yes, and" comes from.

Many years ago, I took a leadership development course that incorporated improv into our training. It was fascinating to learn how an acting technique could improve working relationships and my leadership approach, and yet it makes so much sense. Managers have to learn to navigate through unexpected challenges and make decisions to move the company forward, while engaging others in the process and vision.

The instructor introduced the concept of "Yes, and," where you build on whatever was said prior in the conversation. It's a chance to both move something toward the positive and build on what is being shared. This has now been fully infused in my professional and personal life and has positively changed all communications. It requires you to be fully present and have the mindset to collaborate.

Here's what it sounds like:

Colleague: I think we should try this new strategy for our team.

You: Yes, and we can use this strategy to help reach the goal we talked about in our annual planning process.

Using the structure of "Yes, and," you add your idea to the other person's idea in a way that shows you listened and value what they've shared. When used correctly, it's a powerful technique to introduce to your team so everyone can safely engage in offering their thoughts knowing that others will build on them and have their back.

The more I have incorporated this into my approach, the more I have seen "Yes, and!" emerge in other aspects of my thinking— and my writing. I have noticed far more yeses in my emails to show that I'm affirming the other person's idea or perspective. I might even go so far as to say that all these yeses help me feel more positive overall in my day.

To be clear, though: the idea is not to say yes to everything, just because. An inauthentic "Yes, and" can land the same as a "Yes, but," so this takes real practice and listening.

Also, you may disagree with what's been shared, and there's no value in pretending. You can use "Yes, and" effectively and have a different viewpoint. The key is to first show that you listened to and value the other person's contributions.

Here's what that sounds like:

Colleague: I think we should try this new strategy for our team.

You: Yes, I understand that strategy has worked in your previous work environment, and we can look at the data to inform what we do here. If we proceed, I think we should give ourselves six months to see how it goes and then reevaluate.

It would have been easier to say, "Yes, but that won't work here," and the other person might have shut down immediately because they didn't feel heard. Plus, just because something hasn't worked in the past doesn't mean it won't work now.

"Yes, and" helps you more fully consider new ideas and be open to possibilities.

Find What's Missing

While you're considering new ideas, find ways to bring them to the surface. One of my favorite strategies to get feedback from a group or individual is to ask, What's missing?

Though you may feel a strong affinity with your idea or plan, it's important to hear feedback from stakeholders and others it will affect. The challenge is how to get team members to share candid feedback, especially when it doesn't align with their boss's idea. When you ask, "What's missing?" as a leader, you acknowledge that your idea isn't complete, but it could be if everyone played a role in its development. This makes your team members feel included and more comfortable pointing out issues or seeking clarification. When your team offers input, they will also feel increased buy-in for the concept.

The "what's missing" process is especially valuable when developing new strategies or preparing to launch a new program or process, so you can develop the best possible solutions alongside your team.

147

Admit When You Don't Know

We've been trained to think leaders know exactly what they're doing all the time. (They don't!) Get comfortable saying, "I don't know" to your team when you don't know the answer. It's far better than making something up. It's okay to not have all the answers. Really, it is. Your job is to teach what you can and commit to figuring out the rest with your team. You're human, and being the best boss means showing vulnerability. It will help your team relate to you and feel more invested in what you're building together.

If you want to make a positive impression in a tricky situation, tell them you don't know the answer, but that you'll look into it, and then follow through. Better yet, say, "Let's figure this out together."

Structure Conversations to Promote Transparent Dialogue

It's always beneficial to have collaborative, transparent dialogue with your direct reports, and as your team grows and you become a manager of managers, you'll need to identify creative strategies to interact with team members you don't see as frequently. Though you may be in the same room in large group meetings, you can and should create ways to stay connected and understand how things are going for them at work and beyond.

With all of the responsibilities you already have as a leader, it helps to designate time for these kinds of interactions with team members and structure the conversations to promote dialogue. A skip level meeting is when a higher-level manager meets with employees who report to people they manage or others on their team who don't report directly to them. The goal is to create open lines of communication with the higher-level manager and get insights on what's happening in the organization at all levels. It also helps build relationships with staff who don't report directly to you.

A skip level meeting can be structured in different ways to suit your style and the size of your team. You might choose to organize small groups or meet individually with staff members. And you can decide on whether the cadence will be quarterly or biannually. When you're getting started, you don't have to have all of the details figured out. What matters most is your messaging about why these meetings—and the people in them—are important to you. Don't forget to notify your direct reports about your plans, so they understand up front about your intentions—and you can dispel any worries they might have about what (or who) you'll be talking about in the meeting.

If you're like me and the term "skip level" doesn't resonate with who you are, pick a new name. I had a contest for my team to propose alternate names, and there were many fun options. I chose "elevator sessions"—which both reminded me of the elevator conversations you would serendipitously have with senior leaders and the importance of meeting people literally where they are. The more aligned you feel with this concept, the more your team will see your authentic interest in engaging with them.

For the meeting itself, you are the host, so you'll need to curate the discussion. Establish any expectations and boundaries up front. I liked to explain that I had some questions in mind for them and they could ask me anything on their mind, too. Have an opening question to get everyone more comfortable talking with each other (especially if they're in a group with team members they don't know as well). If you have a well-established team, you may find that they come prepared with questions for you. (I've been asked about what my self-care routine is as often as I've been asked about hybrid work arrangements!)

Here are some additional questions to help guide these conversations:

- What is something the team is doing really well right now?
- What are the barriers or bottlenecks you're experiencing?

- What do you need to be successful?
- What's one thing I should stop or start doing to help the team be more successful?
- What needs clarifying?
- What do I need to know as this team's leader?

If the team members shared something they need help with or more information on, you're accountable as the leader for following up with them in some way. Your follow-through as a leader will determine whether they feel they can come to you again with things they need. Even if you can't change everything they asked about, make sure they feel heard and acknowledged.

In addition to how these meetings help build stronger connections with team members, one of the unexpected benefits was how they helped team members foster relationships with *each other*. Through asking and answering questions that require a level of vulnerability and candor, it increased trust and respect across the group. Research shows that building connections between team members leads to stronger job satisfaction and less burnout—all of which is especially important in hybrid work environments.[6]

INCLUSIVE LEADERSHIP

Inclusive leadership means managing a team as a collective while honoring each individual's unique qualities and experiences. At its essence, it helps individuals feel they belong. This is more than a nice-to-have on a team. Research shows that it contributes to productivity, collaboration, and decision-making.[7] Most important, though, it makes everyone on your team feel valued, just as they should be.

I know this from my own personal experience earlier in my career. I excitedly started a new role, which included participation in leadership meetings (the proverbial "table" where we all want to sit). In my very first meeting, our boss opened with a religious devotional. (For context, we worked for a secular organization.) I felt my face flush, and I glanced around to see if anyone noticed my discomfort. I had worked so hard to finally be in the room where big decisions were made, and as a proud Jewish woman, I immediately felt excluded. I felt unsure how to broach the topic—and it threw me off-balance for contributing at all. Because I was new and I wanted people to accept me, I didn't say anything. To my boss's credit, they approached me a few days after the second meeting and asked if I was okay with the religious discussion. I took a deep breath and was able to share my feelings. They ended up adjusting the meeting to not begin with the weekly devotional, and I started to feel more comfortable speaking up across the board.

Here's the thing: this person is still one of my favorite bosses. We are human and we lead the best ways we can, and we keep learning so we can serve better.

Since then, I've understood I have a responsibility as a leader to create an inclusive culture where my team members feel like they belong and are welcome to share feedback. The work doesn't end when someone finally gets to the table—it begins.

If you're looking to create an inclusive culture within your organization, here are some things to keep in mind.

Model Vulnerability

You model for your team what appropriate norms are, including how to talk about difficult topics at work. I've made it a practice to share my thinking and reasoning with my team, acknowledge my own mistakes, and talk about what I'm working on. While this may start in the little moments in individual conversations, it's also important that you're prepared to lead in the bigger moments, too.

In 2018, the *Chronicle of Philanthropy* announced on the front page that one in four fundraisers had experienced sexual harassment at work, primarily from donors.[8] I brought my team together to talk about this article so they could hear me say that their safety and well-being always comes before the work. We had a candid conversation about strategies to make our profession safer and how to respond if they ever personally felt uncomfortable in a situation. I also opened up about my own personal experience as one of those statistics.

At other significant moments in time, like after George Floyd's murder, I brought the team together to process, share, and learn. In each experience, I acknowledged that I didn't have all the words to address what was happening in the world, but the words I did have were, "We're in this together." Leaders need to open the doors for dialogue, even when they don't have all the words, and understand that their team members might not have the words they need either, but they still need support.

People often ask me how to know if they're disclosing too much. Some of this is learned from experience. For me, I make the choice to determine, "Will this help me build a relationship or connect more genuinely with this person?" Even after all this time of practicing, it doesn't come easily. I still find myself consciously choosing how to show up in this way.

It's okay to not have all the answers or get everything right the first time (or second time) as a leader. Your team wants to relate to you, so help them do that by being willing to talk about your own learning and mistakes.

Make It Safe for People to Speak Up

When you've done the important work to bring diverse perspectives and backgrounds to the table, but then people don't feel safe to share their voice in a discussion, everyone misses out. Though psychological safety is an important factor, it's not the only one. Your team members also have to feel they can make a Bold Move and offer their viewpoints, even if they differ from yours. You can foster this environment by trying out different ways to solicit their feedback and praising when they take a risk to present a new way of thinking or a project to improve your team's work.

This also means you'll have to challenge any behaviors that don't contribute to an inclusive work environment. If you notice a team member who shuts down another person speaking, intentionally or unintentionally, redirect the conversation to amplify the person who was shut down. Say something like, "Patrice, I'm not sure you were quite finished saying your comment, and I'm sure the group would like to hear more of your thoughts."

Even in the safest environments, it will be harder for some people to speak during group dialogue. Find ways to incorporate all voices in a conversation, such as having team members share their thoughts in writing before a meeting, have the group work together on a document in real time, or ask some team members about their thoughts privately to solicit their ideas on how to involve more people in the discussion.

Manage Your Team the Way They Want to Be Managed

Some management articles say things like "Be the boss you wish you had" or "Manage according to the Golden Rule." Giving your team everything you dream of might seem to make sense as a way to pay things forward, but it will miss the mark.

I know this personally because it's how I approached my early managerial roles. There was the time I quietly negotiated for an employee's new title to reflect his increased responsibilities. I was delighted to share this news and recognition, and though he was appreciative, his motivation was increased salary, not title. I wasn't able to get that for him, and we both ended up being disappointed.

Being inclusive means respecting what's important to people—and the best way to understand this is to ask. As a leader, I created a document that all of the employees on my team filled out shortly after onboarding. Among other things, they indicate their preferred ways to be recognized (publicly or privately), what motivates them, and even what their favorite snacks are, so we can understand our individual employees' work styles and customize how we support (and feed) them.

Seek to understand who your team members are as people, what their needs and values are, as well as their strengths. Your job as a leader is to manage your team members the way they want to be managed—and stretch them to fulfill their potential.

Recognize That Inclusion Is Only the Beginning

The first step of being inclusive is acknowledging a person's heritage, religion, or perspective—and there's more to do to help people feel like they truly belong. Here's one example of what this looks like in day-to-day life at work: celebrating a history and culture month is great, but what will you do to create a work environment where people feel valued throughout every single day of the year?

I observe the major Jewish holidays, and each year I take vacation days to honor them. (Speaking of real inclusion, it would be amazing if organizations were more flexible so that people didn't have to use their precious paid time off to be their truest self, but that's another story!) I feel obliged to help people understand when the Jewish holidays are, so they don't schedule important work meetings or send external emails on those days to people who may also be observing. As much as I know this is important, it creates work for me. Just when I finally thought I'd helped our office become more aware, I started to receive multiple emails with project deadlines on the day after the holiday. While that was certainly better than a deadline on the holiday itself, it didn't feel like a recognition of or respect for the significance of the time away and how all deadlines would be affected.

The true difference between inclusion and belonging is seen in how an organization evolves its behaviors to create a meaningful connection to each individual. When people belong, they bring their whole selves—and their best ideas—to work.

Inclusive leadership is a process and an ongoing responsibility, and it is worth your time and effort. When your staff members feel valued and trusted, and more able to be their truest selves at work, the benefits abound. In addition to the research that shows they'll be more deeply engaged in the work, they'll also feel like they belong. As leaders, this should be why we do this work.

BOLD MOVES TO MAKE NOW

Write your About Me document using the template provided in this chapter and share it with your team.

Identify at least one strategy you will use to show appreciation to your team members this week.

Practice one of the courageous communication tips to help your team share feedback with you.

Your Bold Move Community

As you prepare to make your Bold Move journey, it's especially important to consider who you want (and need) by your side along the way. Your journey will be more successful—and more joyful— with the right people supporting, guiding, and inspiring you.

Shawn Achor, author of *The Happiness Advantage* and professor at Harvard Business School, affirms that your social connections are one of the greatest predictors of your success and happiness.[1] That's exactly why we focused on finding advisors and advocates to influence your career earlier in this book. But it's more than just the people you surround yourself with at work. It's about who you bring with you every day, too.

Your Bold Move Community is made up of the people you invest in and who invest in you. This Community includes your support networks, your family, your friends, your partner/spouse, and the next generation. Nurturing relationships with people within your Community is a Bold Move.

What your Community looks like will be deeply personal to you. You may not bring all of these groups with you at the same time. In some cases, you may not bring a particular group with you at all on your journey. When you make your Bold Moves and feel supported along the way, those will be the people who are right for you.

So let's explore the different parts of your Bold Move Community—and learn how we can nurture them for happiness and success (for you and them!).

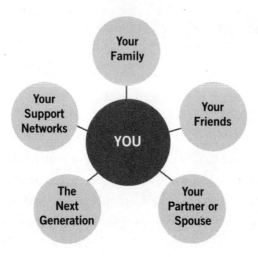

YOUR SUPPORT NETWORKS

A support network, which I define as "a group of people who are aligned around a specific shared interest," can help you achieve your personal and professional goals. The group can be formally organized or informally gathered, and they're different from friends in that they're focused on a particular subject area or topic—which can range from women entrepreneurs to working moms to runners to writers, and more. Everyone needs at least one support network, though I recommend having several.

Think about it. If you want to climb the career ladder, you connect with advisors and advocates in the workplace. If you're building a business, you connect with other entrepreneurs to learn from and offer support. If you're raising a family, you connect with other parents to talk to and ask for advice. Those connections are all helpful for specific and different scenarios. You wouldn't necessarily want to rely on the same person for their insights on parenting and starting a business. For that reason, you have to create support networks to nurture *all* of who you are.

To get started in understanding who comprises this important aspect of your Bold Move Community, jot down a list of the support networks you're already a part of and the individuals you rely on within those networks. To get even deeper, I recommend having two columns on your list: the network or individual's name and what superpower of theirs helps you the most.

If you notice that specific areas of your support networks are not as comprehensive as you would like them to be, make a plan to start building them up. When doing that, consider how each group contributes to and promotes your growth—this will help you find the right people. And when you're ready to meet new people, you can connect through volunteering, sports leagues, and faith communities, among other groups.

It's important to point out that women specifically need their own types of networks to be successful, too. Women-specific communities offer distinct benefits and tend to make those involved feel more empowered and willing to rely on others for social support.[2] In fact, one of my favorite stats shows that of the more than 2,500 women who attend a women's focused conference (specifically the Conferences for Women), 42 percent received a promotion and 15 percent received a pay raise of more than 10 percent.[3] If that doesn't show the power of a women's support groups, I don't know what will!

In addition to women-focused networks, it's also critical that you have access to a more diverse network of people who are not necessarily like you, which exposes you to varied perspectives and access to higher-level opportunities.[4]

Let me be clear: this is more than networking. This is building a support network—a true and important part of *your Community*. While the people in these groups may help you with your professional interests, sometimes even more important, they will be there for you personally as you grow through your experiences, too.

When I think about my own support network, I recall the same group of women who I turned to when I received multiple rejections from my first book proposal: four women I had met once. We initially spoke for a few hours at a professional women's event, and after that we had a lunch here and a dinner there, but I didn't know them for years like my other dear friends, and they didn't know my whole life story. Yet we connected around a specific topic, and their superpowers of being ambitious women entrepreneurs who had also faced rejection were exactly what I needed in that moment and so many other moments since.

YOUR FAMILY

Your journey to who you are today started well before you picked up this book. It started before you even knew what a career was. When you were growing up, the very first people who were alongside you were your family members.

Who was the first person to tell you, "I believe in you"? That voice is often the one we internalize over time to believe in ourselves. I'm fortunate that I had many people in my family to encourage me at every stage of my life to pursue what I dreamed of, and I hope the same for you. This doesn't, however, mean they agreed with every choice I made; rather, they gave me the foundation to make choices for myself.

Family relationships throughout your life are linked to well-being,[5] and positive relationships with your parents affect your motivation and work ethic.[6] That said, family means something different to each person, and families can be complicated.

As I grew up, family meant driving back and forth two hours each way between my parents' homes every weekend (they divorced when I was six). I joked to friends that I had two different lives and the best of both worlds, but it was also hard to constantly feel pulled in multiple directions. Gratefully, one consistent thing was that I always felt loved. My family includes my siblings, Shira and Danny. Though I wasn't always as close with them as children (I'm the big sister), I have become inseparable with them now and love knowing them as adults.

Your family structure may include parents, grandparents, siblings, godparents, aunts, uncles, cousins, and others. No matter who makes up your family unit, I hope you always felt and feel loved too.

Your family connections also factor into your career, leadership, and personal growth. Research shows that parental support, particularly in adolescence, plays a significant role in their children's future career exploration.[7] Looking back: How has your family (parents or others) encouraged your Bold Moves? What do you wish they would have done differently to counsel or guide you?

While you can't control the family situation you were born into or the level of support you received from your family, you can make choices about what you want now and seek it out from your family members or others you call family. Some of the challenges between adult children and parents have to do with managing each other's expectations. Stew Friedman of the Wharton School suggests an exercise where children write out why their parents matter to them and what they believe their parents' expectations are of them, and then the children and parents discuss the answers.[8] Friedman reports parents were generally more supportive and accepting than anticipated. The stories we write for ourselves may not be accurate, and this kind of open dialogue gives families a chance to rewrite the story they want. Your family may have shaped who you were, but ultimately you will determine who you want to become.

Now let's talk about the people who may just turn into family.

YOUR FRIENDS

You already know how vital friendships are to your life. Your friends are the individuals who are there for you when you need them, they support you in your best and most challenging moments, and they inspire you to be your truest self.

In addition to the way you *feel* when you're with friends, research studies show that friendship has many quantifiable benefits, including reducing your stress levels,[9] boosting your self-esteem,[10] and positively affecting your health outcomes.[11] In one study, friendships played a more important role in long-term well-being than strong family connections—and this well-being predictor was particularly true for women.[12]

At different stages in your life, friendship will look and feel different. After you graduate from college, you generally reduce your inner circle of friends, and this will continue throughout your adult life. Friendships will evolve and so will you. You don't need to get caught up in how many friends you have. In fact, researchers have mixed results on the number of friends you need to have to feel fulfilled (some say one, others three to five,[13] and another showed as many as 150![14]). That being said, you should determine what number feels right based on your personality, and what makes you feel included and supported. Also, since there are many facets of you, you should seek out different types of friends to support you. The goal here is to feel like you *belong* somewhere, because loneliness has negative effects on your physical and mental health.[15]

Maintaining friendships can be a challenge when you're focused on growing your career, yet research shows this is exactly when you should focus on your relationships. A study discussed in *Science Daily* shows that highly motivated individuals are more inclined to pursue personal growth goals when they feel supported by people who care about them.[16] Making time for friends is part of how you invest in yourself, so let's discuss the ways you can do that now.

Put in the Effort

Friendships require effort to sustain, so make plans to see friends and show up. Be present when you're with them. Support them with their wins and their setbacks. Share what's happening in your life, even the difficult things, and invite them to do the same.

According to Shasta Nelson, a friendship expert and author of *The Business of Friendship*, friendships thrive on three elements: positivity, consistency, and vulnerability.[17] And it's important to point out here that consistency is different from frequency. You absolutely can preserve a special friendship with someone you don't see often or who lives far away—you just have to be committed to meaningful connection points along the way. Schedule a catch-up call every few months, reach out when something reminds you of them, or send a handwritten note to celebrate a special milestone. Some of the best friends are the people you can have a conversation with after months or years and it feels like no time has passed at all.

Create New Relationships

It is possible to make friends as an adult, though it can feel harder. Among other reasons, you may feel nervous to socially approach people you don't know as well or believe you don't have enough time to develop a new relationship.[18] Let's remember the Bold Move we committed to in Chapter 5 is creating a moment of genuine connection with others. Initiate a conversation with the person you regularly see at the coffee shop. Invite your new colleague for lunch or a walk. Say yes to an after-work invitation even if you're tired or you have planned to binge-watch your favorite show. Like most Bold Moves, you'll have to put yourself out there and follow through without knowing whether it will lead to your desired goal—but the end result may turn out even better than you expected.

Know When to Let Go

As important as it is to spend time building friendships, it's also valuable to know when to let go (and have the strength to do so).

While letting go can be incredibly difficult, focus your energy and time on the people in your life who show up for you. Someone once shared the idea that some friends are in your life for a reason, a season, or lifetime, and it is my hope that this idea helps you understand that not every friendship has to be for life—and that's okay. I know it has helped me.

Every step of this Bold Move journey is for learning, and who you choose to take these steps with you can meaningfully contribute to your success and happiness. Prioritize people who value you, stretch you to grow, and bring you joy.

Now let's move to the family you create for yourself.

YOUR PARTNER OR SPOUSE

Matt and I met when we were only 17. A week before high school graduation, I noticed him at a tennis club where he worked while I accompanied a friend. Though he and I didn't speak at the time, we ran into each other a few weeks later in Outer Banks, North Carolina, where our respective high schools were vacationing for Beach Week.

Matt and I dated long distance all throughout college between North Carolina and New York City. We fell in love with each other just as we were discovering who we were as people—and who we wanted to become. During that time, we both became clear on what we wanted our (separate) careers to be, but one thing we didn't make clear was how we were going to navigate them together.

I can still remember our first conversation (read: argument) about our careers as we applied for our dream jobs in different cities as seniors in college. It was the beginning of many, many discussions about how we would grow our careers while we grew our relationship, and eventually a family.

Matt and I are what is called a "dual career couple," which is essentially when both people in a partnership have jobs. We (perhaps naively) presumed we would both have ambitious careers, but we didn't initially discuss how this was actually going to play out. We hadn't considered that having two demanding careers might require additional support at home, or that there are other options, such as some couples take turns pursuing their career goals and other couples choose careers with different or complementary work schedules. Multiple options can be effective for dual career couples, but the dependent factor is whether or not the couple designs the model together in a way that works for both people.

Today, Matt and I have built a framework that allowed us to create a life together that we truly love and careers we are incredibly proud of. I'd love to share that with you so you can find what works for you, too.

Clarify Expectations

For you and your partner to create a model that works for both of you, you'll need to have open conversations about your expectations for what you envision your life to be like and how you'll make it work. Talking through your partnership could include your personal values, your short- and long-term professional goals, what you hope to accomplish in your career, and anything else you need to discuss related to what you envision for your life. How you'll make it work details include which areas of the country or world could work (or not), how much business travel will be acceptable, whether you're both going to work full-time or part-time, how you will handle money, childcare (if you think you may want to have children), which responsibilities are whose, and everything in between.

One thing I have to call out, though: be prepared to flex, and be willing to compromise in order to support both parties' goals and dreams.

I'm fairly certain I said I would never move to Alabama—and yet we still ended up living there for five years while my husband pursued his doctorate. Situations like this can easily devolve into whose career is more "important." (I felt like I was taking a step back in order for him to pursue his goals.) But when you've talked through and clarified your expectations together, it becomes easier to reframe almost any situation into an opportunity for both of you. (In our case, I eventually found a job that positioned me well for the rest of my career and worked for someone who would be one of my best bosses ever, Pam.)

Coordinate Schedules

In your commitment to continual conversation with your partner about time and priorities, I recommend establishing weekly
or monthly meetings to look at your calendars and handle potential conflicts. There's nothing quite like realizing you both have an
early meeting or need to travel at the same time—the morning of.
Technology can help you with these conversations by using apps to
track your shared calendars and to-do lists and discussing who is
best suited for which tasks at home. (You could even talk through
money at the same time!)

Prioritize Time

Your time is limited, so spend it wisely. If something will pull you
away from your family, choose activities that energize you and
bring you extra joy. You'll especially have to prioritize your time
when you're a caregiver. This means saying no to the opportunities
that don't serve you at the life moment you're in, whether that's the
teacher-school association, nonprofit committee, or a gala event.
Saying no to something allows you to say yes to what matters most
to you—like the commitments you've made to invest in yourself.

Here are some questions to ask yourself to help you decide
whether or not you should take on a new project or activity:

1. Does this use your superpowers and/or create new learning
   that you would value?
2. Will you feel this is a meaningful use of your time?
3. How will this affect your work and home life?

I've had to get very good at knowing what I want so I can proactively seek out those projects and say no to the many other invitations. Saying no to a project doesn't have to mean forever. Know
what your limit is at one time and revisit for the future.

Support Each Other

Research shows that power dynamics in a relationship can be a challenge when it comes to dual career couples.[19] Household responsibilities often cause strife because they're yet another thing that has to be done after a full day of work. Having open communication about roles and expectations can help avoid frustration and resentment. People tend to inflate what they do and minimize other people's contributions in their minds. (This is actual psychology, not spouse science!)

Tiffany Dufu's *Drop the Ball* and Eve Rodsky's *Fair Play* are helpful books on how to communicate with your partner about what your priorities are and how to divide household responsibilities. Also consider what you can delegate or outsource, so you can focus on your best and highest use of time.

Supporting each other goes beyond the to-do list. It's also about being present for each other. People have a universal need to feel heard, reinforcing the importance of active listening at home. Do not try to guess what the other person is thinking or why they're doing something. (I am very good at writing a story, but it's not always the right story!) Ask questions and listen. Proactively develop a plan together for how you and your partner will connect with each other, particularly if you have children with their own needs and schedules. For example, you may decide you'll call each other on the commute home to talk before the rush of the evening obligations, you'll spend the first 15 minutes at home talking through the day, or you prefer to wait until after the kids go to bed. After you've decided the timing that works best for you, make a point to listen to your partner's stories and worries from work.

Outside of your evening catch-ups, which can be thwarted by work and family demands, schedule time for just the two of you, whether a recurring weekly date night or a shared activity. Matt and I exercise together several days a week and plan early morning dates at our favorite coffee shop.

Jennifer Petriglieri, a professor at INSEAD and author of *Couples That Work*, suggests that the most successful working couples both support and push each other. When you experience a setback or challenge, it's natural to want your spouse to respond compassionately. On *Harvard Business Review*'s *Women at Work* podcast, Petriglieri references research that shows you also fare better when your spouse thoughtfully asks you what you plan to change about the situation and what you will do going forward.[20] They aren't checking up to see if you did it, they're encouraging you to do it—that's what makes the difference.

Talk with your partner about how you can support each other in being your best selves. My mantra as a working parent: I'm doing the best I can every day. Your best self doesn't mean perfect!

I'm fortunate to have an incredibly supportive husband who believes in me and my career as much as his own—and I know he can say the same for me. You already know your partner will be an important part of your life. Who you choose as your partner will be one of the most important *career* decisions you'll make, too.

THE NEXT GENERATION

One of my mom friends reached out to me for advice on how to help support her child who was considering running for student government election. Her child was nervous that no one would vote for her and wasn't sure it was worth putting herself out there. I offered to connect with my friend's daughter, whom I've known since she and my son were toddlers. I wasn't sure the young woman would want to take me up on the offer. I mean, she was a middle schooler, and of course, grown-ups don't know all that much according to them. To my surprise, she said she would be willing to talk with me, and I was glad she did.

While we were on the phone, I asked her about the issues that were most important to her, why she was the best person for the role, and how she would serve her classmates well. She had well-formed answers and spoke with true conviction about why her voice matters. I was so moved to hear a young woman speaking about herself in this way.

I told her the story about what it was like for me when I ran for student government when I was in middle school. For weeks after school, I planned my campaign. I found a perfect walk-up song that had my name in it and designed earrings that read "Shanna for President." On the day of the election, I stood on stage in front of hundreds of peers. I could barely see over the podium. I read my speech and played "Get a Job," a song by Sha Na Na (the lyrics of the chorus sound like my name on repeat) on my tape recorder I had lugged up there with me. Though I could hear several kids laughing (and their jokes the rest of the day), I smiled proudly anyway. Later that day, I learned I didn't win the election.

Here's the thing: this story is the first thing I thought of 30 years later when my friend mentioned middle school elections. In my experience, it wasn't the hurt feelings I remembered so much as the pride in my confidence to unabashedly pursue what was important to me, even at a younger age. I hoped that one day my friend's child would feel the same way, whichever way the outcome went for her. As I recalled this story, I coached the young woman that this is a reminder of why you need to keep putting yourself out there, even if things don't go as hoped or planned every time. Because you will have to continue to use your voice for what is important to you, even if others criticize you.

As we are on our own journeys to commit to putting our best selves out there with one Bold Move a day, it's important to encourage this in our own children or children we care about. Here are four things you can do to cultivate the Bold Move Mindset in children of all ages.

Talk About Your Bold Moves

Explicitly share the steps you're taking to make your own Bold Moves. Even before children can fully understand what's required to get to that point or the potential risk of things not going as hoped, they'll begin to create their own understanding of the roadmap for how to make Bold Moves through your storytelling.

Ask Questions About What They're Feeling (Including Their Fears)

You don't need to dissuade children from whatever they're feeling, even if you don't see it or don't agree with it. Honor their feelings by actively listening, acknowledging their worries, and then ask open-ended questions to better understand where they're coming from. When people feel heard, they're better able to make good decisions.

Show Them What's Possible

The reframe and mindset shift of "What's the *best* that can happen?" works for children as much as it does grownups. Ask them to think about what could go well, encourage them to consider the list of their superpowers, and remind them of their strengths and ability to influence others.

I'm reminded of the story another friend told me about seeing her middle school daughter come downstairs in her mom's Be

Yourself Boldly T-shirt from my shop. When her mom asked about it, the young woman said that it was exactly what she needed for her theater tryouts that day, to remind her to put her best self out there.

Ask a Child About Your Career

Children can teach you, too.

In March 2020, my son, Eli, and I were out for a mother-son dinner date. It ended up being the last time I went out to dinner before the pandemic started.

In between conversations about March Madness, what happened on the playground that day, and how delicious the meal was, I asked Eli what he thought about my career.

It hadn't occurred to me to do this until I was prompted by an author I mentioned earlier, whom I have also been fortunate enough to get better acquainted with over the years, Tiffany Dufu. During a coffee catch-up she and I had a few weeks prior, she asked me what was ahead for me, and I shared my thoughts. Then she asked me what my son thought. I remember being a little incredulous at this question. After all, my son was not quite 11 yet. She assured me she had done this often with her kids, even at younger ages.

In typical Tiffany fashion, she was so right. It ended up being one of the most meaningful conversations with my son—and I've looked back several times at the notes I secretly typed into my phone when he watched the last few minutes of the game on the restaurant TV.

The clarity of Eli's response was breathtaking. He told me to keep working on my side career for two years, to increase the number of people I was reaching. He said that would help me know if I wanted to do that work full-time. I asked him how he would feel about me traveling more frequently again. He said, "If you're happy,

I'm happy." Then he asked me to take him on some of my trips and I promised to.

Children truly are listening and learning, even when they don't show it. So try this with your own children, or children you're close to and who know you well. Ask them:

What do you think about my career?

What do you think I should do next?

What do you think is ahead for me?

Document their responses and the date so you can look back on this in the future. Children take cues from you and how you approach the world. When you model for them what it means to make one Bold Move a day for themselves, you will also find the motivation you need for your own.

• • •

Who you take with you on your Bold Move journey matters—both for your joy and for your success.

BOLD MOVES TO MAKE NOW

Identify a support network you have already and/or aspire to have and reach out to join their next activity.

Reconnect with a friend to share a positive memory, or invite a new friend to coffee.

Tell your children and/or other children you care about one of your stories to inspire them to make their one Bold Move a day.

Conclusion

Putting Your Bold Move Mindset to the Test

I'm so proud of you.

You made it to this point.

You kept showing up for yourself.

You're committed to learning.

You're serving others.

You're finding joy.

Celebrate this progress.

It's time to put your Bold Move Mindset to the test.

You've been practicing with each chapter in your Bold Moves to Make Now. Now you decide what your Bold Moves will be.

As you're out there advancing your career, growing as a person, and developing as a leader, keep in mind the four mindsets

(Gratitude Mindset, Happiness Mindset, *And* Mindset, Progress Mindset) to guide you while you put yourself out there and follow through. Bold Moves are a choice you make each day, though they look different for everyone and even differ day to day. You'll know them when you feel them, the ones that make your heart start to beat a bit faster, and a little voice in your head may tell you to be cautious—and you'll do it anyway. Through the fears. Through the uncertainty. Because you believe in possibility. And you believe in yourself.

Don't be surprised if you find yourself making Bold Moves even more than you expected!

I'm not surprised, though. I believed in you from the start.

• • •

As I reflect on this book, it came from a series of Bold Moves. After spending the early part of 2020 querying agents for a book I had started drafting about women's leadership and being rejected from every single one, I had to accept that my book dream might not happen. That this coincided with the biggest crisis of our lifetimes, the Covid-19 pandemic, wasn't lost on me. After mourning the loss of the book dream for a while, I realized I wasn't going to let other people decide how I could serve women who wanted to level up in their careers and leadership.

One day as I scrolled through Instagram, I saw a call to action from Molly Beck, Founder of Messy.fm and author of *Reach Out*, that said, "Who is a leader that should have their own podcast? Hint: It might be you." I stared at the post for a minute, reflecting on all the times I had considered this before and put it to the side, and commented, "Molly, I'm raising my own hand." Talking with Molly a few weeks later, it was easy to get wrapped up in her enthusiasm for the medium, but as I spoke about my ideas, I realized they were far clearer than I had even realized. As excited as I was to launch the podcast, I had no experience recording or editing. After five weeks of overthinking, rerecording, and some tears, I launched *One Bold Move a Day*, a (then) daily six-minute podcast to help women achieve their goals and advance their careers.

Looking back, I could've raised my hand and then changed my mind. I could've had the initial call and then given up. (Believe me, there were some days where I thought about it.) What kept me going was helping women at a time they needed it most. Day by day, I figured out the podcasting process. I still recorded some episodes multiple times, but I didn't feel as overwhelmed. I felt vulnerable sharing stories I'd never told anyone and hoped the sharing would decrease the stigma for everyone. Though I felt incredibly fulfilled in supporting women through the podcast, the book dream was still on my heart.

So, I pursued it again—and it led me to you.

As I spent time writing this book about what it means to make Bold Moves to advance your career, grow as a person, and develop as a leader, I started to think even more deeply than ever before about what this meant for me personally.

During the pandemic, my identity changed. Perhaps yours did, too. I started to reconsider what was most important to me and, for the first time, truly realized I was more than my work, job, or title.

It was in creating this guide for you that I also found clarity in my own calling. I made the boldest move to leave a career I loved to start my own company full-time. I knew it would allow me to help more organizations and leaders to fulfill their potential.

And yes, I ran toward something. With joy.

As I was considering this move, I mentioned to my friend Ali that I thought the universe was sending me a message, and perhaps I would wait to have everything figured out before I made a full-time career as an entrepreneur. She asked me, "What makes you think the universe is going to make it completely clear for you if you haven't yet fully dedicated yourself to making this choice?" That resonated with me. Bold Moves are more than the act itself— it's the follow-through, too, that will differentiate you.

Friends and colleagues who knew me worried that I would leave behind a career I have been so good at. Here's the thing about what you are very good at, whatever that means for you: when we stop learning, we stop growing.

You can love something with your whole heart and still walk away from it in order to grow. This is who I am meant to become. I couldn't have known it then, but I listened to my heart. (I even walked through the four questions I shared in Chapter 4 about what to consider before taking a new job!)

Through my work, I'm able to partner with more companies and nonprofit organizations to build stronger workplace cultures, develop leaders to reach their potential, and support women to thrive at work. And on most days, I've been able to pick up my son from school, too.

I'm confident the Bold Move Mindset has sustained me through everything up to this point, and I can't wait to see what you have in store for the world when you apply this for yourself.

In the quiet moments when you feel unsure about which direction you should go or your Bold Move Mindset is being tested, come back to this book as a resource. Picture having coffee with me if it helps!

Just as I created this roadmap for your success, I know you'll now create the pathways for other women. You're their leader, their sponsor, their mentor, their friend, their sister, and their cheerleader. You're a role model for how to achieve more than you ever thought possible.

May this be just the beginning of your journey. I am always, always cheering you on.

Notes

CHAPTER 1

1. https://thriveglobal.com/stories/how-practicing-gratitude-can -make-you-more-resilient/.
2. https://www.sciencedirect.com/science/article/abs/pii/S00223999 08004224.
3. https://journals.aom.org/doi/full/10.5465/amj.2016.0594 .summary.

CHAPTER 2

1. https://whitneyjohnson.com/distinctive-strengths/.
2. https://www.newyorker.com/science/maria-konnikova/the-secret -formula-for-resilience.
3. https://www.theatlantic.com/health/archive/2016/05/why-self -compassion-works-better-than-self-esteem/481473/.

CHAPTER 3

1. https://scholar.dominican.edu/cgi/viewcontent.cgi?article=1265 &context=news-releases.
2. Sinek, Simon. *Start With Why: How Great Leaders Inspire Everyone To Take Action.* New York: Penguin Group (2009).

3. https://psycnet.apa.org/doiLanding?doi=10.1037%2F0022-3514 .67.3.366.
4. https://jamesclear.com/habit-stacking.
5. https://psycnet.apa.org/record/2014-02577-006.
6. https://www.ncbi.nlm.nih.gov/pmc/articles/PMC3291107/.
7. https://anderson-review.ucla.edu/emergency-reserves/.
8. https://hbr.org/2011/05/the-power-of-small-wins.
9. https://hbr.org/2011/05/the-power-of-small-wins.

CHAPTER 4

1. https://blog.linkedin.com/2019/september/26/closing-the -network-gap.
2. https://www.ted.com/talks/carla_harris_how_to_find_the_ person_who_can_help_you_get_ahead_at_work.
3. https://hbr.org/2017/02/lifelong-learning-is-good-for-your-health -your-wallet-and-your-social-life.
4. https://qz.com/work/1565548/linkedin-says-women-are-less -likely-to-apply-for-jobs-but-more-likely-to-get-them/.

CHAPTER 5

1. http://time.com/4070299/secret-to-happiness/.
2. https://www.researchgate.net/publication/283087013_Close _Relationships_and_Happiness.
3. https://journals.sagepub.com/doi/abs/10.1177/0956797618783714 ?mod=article_inline.
4. https://journals.sagepub.com/doi/full/10.1177/0963721421100 2538.
5. https://didyouknowfacts.com/theres-now-a-name-for-the-micro -generation-born-between-1977-1983.

CHAPTER 6

1. https://www.themuse.com/advice/5-sciencebacked-reasons-why -readers-do-better-in-their-careers.
2. https://www.forbes.com/sites/ashleystahl/2018/07/25/heres-how -creativity-actually-improves-your-health/#1473a2f813a6.
3. https://link.springer.com/article/10.1007/s10902-018-9976-0.
4. https://www.scientificamerican.com/article/q-a-why-a-rested -brain-is-more-creative/.
5. https://www.ncbi.nlm.nih.gov/pmc/articles/PMC7261660/.
6. https://www.ncbi.nlm.nih.gov/pmc/articles/PMC6585675/.

7. https://www.ncbi.nlm.nih.gov/pmc/articles/PMC5923838/.
8. https://www.ncbi.nlm.nih.gov/pmc/articles/PMC6281147/.
9. https://hbr.org/2018/09/sleep-well-lead-better.
10. https://www.nationalgeographic.com/travel/article/planning-a-trip-is-good-for-you-especially-during-pandemic.
11. https://www.nytimes.com/2015/06/28/travel/tips-for-keeping-that-post-vacation-feeling.html.
12. https://hbr.org/2016/07/the-data-driven-case-for-vacation.
13. https://hbr.org/2016/07/the-data-driven-case-for-vacation.

CHAPTER 7

1. http://www.columbia.edu/~da358/publications/listening_influence.pdf.
2. https://hbr.org/2012/01/positive-intelligence.

CHAPTER 8

1. https://hbr.org/2016/04/research-we-are-way-harder-on-female-leaders-who-make-bad-calls.
2. http://www.boarddiversity.ca/sites/default/files/IJBGE8-Paper5-Why-Women-Make-Better-Directors.pdf.
3. https://journals.sagepub.com/doi/10.2307/3094912.
4. https://www.nytimes.com/2015/08/16/jobs/when-youre-in-charge-your-whisper-may-feel-like-a-shout.html.
5. https://hbr.org/1999/11/management-time-whos-got-the-monkey.
6. https://journals.sagepub.com/doi/pdf/10.1177/1948550616651681.

CHAPTER 9

1. https://www.linkedin.com/pulse/leaders-need-user-manuals-what-i-learned-writing-mine-abby-falik/.
2. https://www.linkedin.com/pulse/20140106124338-35894743-what-if-you-had-to-write-a-user-manual-about-your-leadership-style/.
3. https://thriveglobal.com/stories/compassionate-directness-cultural-value-ultimate-advantage-arianna-huffington/.
4. https://hbr.org/2013/11/be-grateful-more-often.
5. http://people.stern.nyu.edu/jhaidt/articles/vianello.galliani.2010.elevation-at-work.pub081.pdf.
6. https://hbr.org/2017/06/burnout-at-work-isnt-just-about-exhaustion-its-also-about-loneliness.

7. https://hbr.org/2019/03/why-inclusive-leaders-are-good-for -organizations-and-how-to-become-one.

8. https://www.philanthropy.com/article/sexual-harassment-is -widespread-problem-for-fundraisers-survey-shows/.

CHAPTER 10

1. Achor, Shawn. *The Happiness Advantage: The Seven Principles of Positive Psychology That Fuel Success and Performance at Work* (2010).

2. https://www.nature.com/articles/d41586-018-07878-w.

3. https://hbr.org/2018/02/do-womens-networking-events-move-the -needle-on-equality.

4. ttps://hbr.org/2019/02/research-men-and-women-need-different -kinds-of-networks-to-succeed.

5. https://www.ncbi.nlm.nih.gov/pmc/articles/PMC5954612/.

6. https://www.tandfonline.com/doi/full/10.1080/00221309.2016 .1258386.

7. https://www.sciencedirect.com/science/article/abs/pii/S00018791 09000359.

8. https://hbr.org/2016/08/what-to-do-if-your-parents-are-causing -you-career-angst.

9. https://www.ncbi.nlm.nih.gov/pmc/articles/PMC2921311/.

10. https://psycnet.apa.org/fulltext/2019-55803-001.html.

11. https://www.ncbi.nlm.nih.gov/pmc/articles/PMC3150158/.

12. https://onlinelibrary.wiley.com/doi/abs/10.1111/pere.12187.

13. https://www.psychologytoday.com/us/blog/lifetime-connections/ 201908/how-many-friends-do-you-really-need-in-adulthood.

14. https://www.sciencedaily.com/releases/2021/05/210504211054 .htm.

15. https://www.nia.nih.gov/news/social-isolation-loneliness-older -people-pose-health-risks.

16. https://www.sciencedaily.com/releases/2017/09/170925095426. htm.

17. https://www.nytimes.com/2018/01/18/smarter-living/how-to -maintain-friends.html.

18. https://www.sciencedirect.com/science/article/abs/pii/S01918869 20302324.

19. https://hbr.org/2020/02/why-power-couples-need-to-talk-more -about-power.

20. https://hbr.org/podcast/2018/02/couples-that-work.

Acknowledgments

How very fortunate I am to have my own Bold Move Community supporting, guiding, and inspiring me.

To my editor, Cheryl Segura, and the McGraw Hill team, thank you for believing in the power of Bold Moves. Cheryl, it is *bashert* ("meant to be") that we got to work together on this special project. Thank you for helping transform this book into what it is today. Special thanks to the team behind this book: Jonathan Lyons for advocating for me, and Rebecca Proulx and Fortier Public Relations for helping share this message with the world.

I've learned from the best advisors and advocates throughout my life and career. Sharing my deepest gratitude to Dr. Shuly Rubin Schwartz, Bob Shepard, Pam Parker, and Leslie Laird Kruhly for creating pathways for me. Erica Keswin, Molly Beck, and Hitha Palepu, thank you for wholeheartedly embracing the concept of One Bold Move a Day. I admire you for your thought leadership and I value your friendship even more so.

To the colleagues who have become friends. Sara McCord, you were the first person I told my unicorn goal of writing a book, and you coached, challenged, and supported me throughout the process. Shannon Wood, your Bold Move led to us working together, and you are a valued sounding board and champion for One Bold Move a Day.

To the friends who have become like family. Thank you to Leora Eisenstadt, my HeyMama PHL support network (Ronica Cleary, Christy MacGregor, Elizabeth McNevin, and Jenny Meassick), and MNO (Analisa Halpern, Bindu Kumar, Jenny Pahys, Jordana Popovich, and Emily Stewart) for your support in navigating motherhood and our biggest career dreams.

To my family. Mom, the many ways you've believed in me helped me learn how to believe in myself. You're my mirror, cheerleader, and role model. Dad, you modeled work/life integration before it was even a thing people talked about, imparted the importance of *tzedakah* ("philanthropy"), and brought books to life, all of which became essential components of who I am. To my beloved siblings, Shira Ackerman and Chris Pecoraro, and Danny and Stefanie Ackerman, our adventures together are some of my favorite memories, and as our beloved song says: who you're with is what matters most. To my parents-in-law, Marilyn Hocking and Brian Hocking, thank you for welcoming me into your lives on the day we met.

To Eli, I'm so proud to be your mother. May you continue to make Bold Moves throughout your life and career—the world will be better for it. Love you mostest. To Matt, my husband, my partner, and my best friend. When we met at 17, I couldn't have dreamed of the dual careers, family, and joy we would create together. I'm grateful for your support and encouragement to make my Bold Moves and be my truest self every day. Our life together is my favorite Bold Move.

Index

About the Author

Shanna A. Hocking (Shanna rhymes with Donna) is a leadership consultant, philanthropic advisor, and keynote speaker with 20 years of experience raising hundreds of millions of dollars and leading large teams at organizations such as the Wharton School of the University of Pennsylvania, Children's Hospital of Philadelphia, University of Alabama, and Duke University.  Her clients include universities, national nonprofit organizations, global businesses, and family foundations. She also is the host of the popular business podcast *One Bold Move a Day*. Her expertise has been featured in *Harvard Business Review, Entrepreneur, Chicago Tribune, Today.com, Insider, The Muse, Fast Company, Motherly*, and *Thrive Global*, among others. She lives in the Philadelphia suburbs with her husband and son.

ShannaAHocking.com
Instagram: @ShannaAHocking
LinkedIn: LinkedIn.com/in/ShannaAHocking